Genesis Curriculum

Giant Leap

Second Edition

Second Edition

Welcome to Giant Leap, the third book in Genesis Curriculum's Steps series. This book is aimed at children ages 5 and 6. If you have an older child who needs more work with learning to read, consider using Easy Peasy's Learn to Read course, also available in book form, so your child doesn't have all the math and activities for younger children. This course will take your child from being a beginning reader to being able to read novels. It will guide your child through learning to write letters, numbers, and words. Children will count and identify numbers to one hundred, work on addition and subtraction facts, and be introduced to the concepts of money, time, and fractions. Basic math skills like skip counting, patterns, and using a number line are practiced, and word problems are used to apply learning.

Each day there are two pages (until the very end of the book). Each day there is one reading page and one activity page. There are 180 days of activities.

A little how-to guidance:

For reading they will be working through the McGuffey First Reader as well as having interspersed phonics lessons. The McGuffey stories have a list of new words. Read over those words with your child. If they come to one of those words in the story and don't know it, practice with them using the list, and then let them try the sentence again. Any phonics concept they've learned, such as SH or EA, they can sound out if they are stuck on a word. It's okay to give them any word they can't sound out and don't know. Point to the word and say it. Then have them read the sentence or that part of the sentence again with the word in it. There are some stories that you will read over a couple of days. Often I have the whole story on the second page with an asterisk marking where you left off in the story. On these pages my son and I read out loud simultaneously up to the new part.

With handwriting you can read over the directions with your child and then demonstrate the first letter. Have your child circle their best one.

Read together the math directions and have your child do the activity. I have always sat with my child for reading and math, demonstrated the handwriting, and then left him to work alone at that point. For math I wrote in the answers the first half of the year. They will be learning most of the addition and subtraction facts, apart from some of the upper ones. They will use patterns to figure out some of those higher answers like 8 + 8 and 9 + 9. They don't have to have the facts mastered by memory. Help them count on by starting with the largest number and then using their fingers to count on the smaller number. For instance, if it's seven plus three, you would put up three fingers. You start at seven and then touch each finger and count 8 – 9 – 10. They will do a little with coins, time, and fractions. These aren't concepts that need to be mastered right now. It's just a first look at them.

Day 1

Drawing

Draw a picture of yourself writing. This year you're going to learn to write words, sentences, and numbers.

Counting to 20

Use the number line to count up to 20. Touch each number as you say it. One, two, ... Then count backwards from 20 using the number line. 20, 19, ...

a e i o u

u o i e a

e o a i u

o i e u a

i a u e o

Read the short vowel sounds of the letters, NOT their names. Read "a" as in "hat," "e" as in "bed," "i" as in "hit," "o" as in "hot," "u" as in "sun." This is how you will read these vowels in the coming phonics lessons as well.

Day 2

Uppercase L

Write an L in each box. Start near the middle of the top of the box. Draw a line straight down to the bottom. Draw the line over to the right edge of the box. Circle your best one.

Counting to 20

Today count to 20. Count out loud just saying the numbers. Then count the pictures below. Then count objects. Do it at least five times. What can you find twenty of in your house to practice counting?

Have your child say the B sound "buh", then the short vowel sound, then the two together. Don't read "be" as in "bee"; read "be" as in "bed."

b	a	ba
b	e	be
b	i	bi
b	o	bo
b	u	bu

Day 3

Uppercase T

Write a T in each box. Start on the top middle of the box. Draw a line down to the bottom. Jump up to the top and draw a line from one corner to the other. We JUMP back up to the top instead of drawing another line back up because it's hard to draw right on top of your first line. Circle your best one.

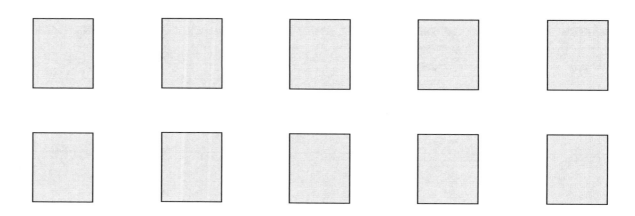

Skip Counting By 2

Circle every other number, starting with 2. Then read those numbers to count to 20 by twos. These are called the **even** numbers. Then try to count to 20 by twos without reading the list below.

1 2 3 4 5 6 7 8 9 10

11 12 13 14 15 16 17 18 19 20

Dd

Remember to read the vowels with their short vowel sound. Don't read "do" as in "doo"; read "do" as in "dot."

d a   da

d e   de

d i   di

d o   do

d u   du

ba di bu de bo

Day 4

Uppercase I

Write an I in each box. Start on the top middle of the box. Draw a line to the bottom of the box. Jump back up to the top. Draw a line across the top of the box. Then jump to the bottom and draw a line across the bottom of the box. Circle your best one.

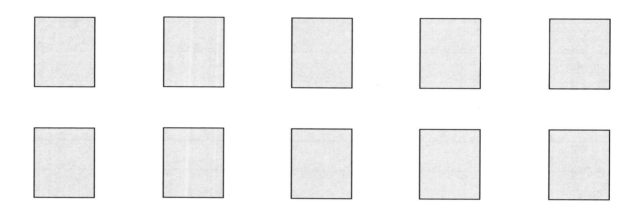

Skip Counting By 2

Circle every other number, starting with 1. Then read those numbers to count to 20 by twos. These are called the **odd** numbers. Then try to count to 20 by twos without reading the list below.

1 2 3 4 5 6 7 8 9 10

11 12 13 14 15 16 17 18 19 20

Have your child read the first and second letters individually, using their sounds, not names, and making sure to use the short vowel sounds. Then combine them when they are read together on the right.

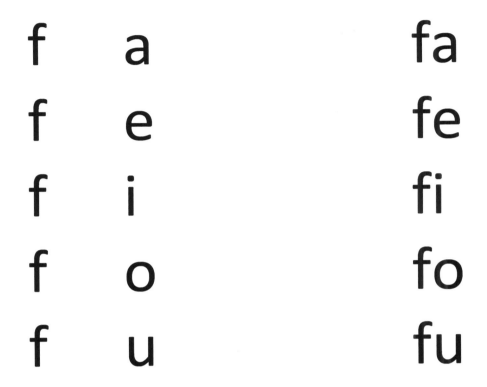

f	a		fa
f	e		fe
f	i		fi
f	o		fo
f	u		fu

ba   fi   di   bu   fe

do   de   bo   fu

da   fo   be

Day 5

Uppercase F

Write an F in each box. Start in the top corner of the box. Draw a line to the bottom of the box. Jump back up to the top of the box. Draw a line across the top of the box. Jump down to the middle of the box. Draw a line from one side of the box to almost the whole way across the box. Circle your best one.

Even Numbers

Circle pairs of footprints like the example. Every circle will have two footprints in them. Count how many footprints by skip counting by two. 2, 4,... Since every footprint has its pair, there are an **even** number of footprints.

Read the consonant sound, then the short vowel sound, and then the two combined.

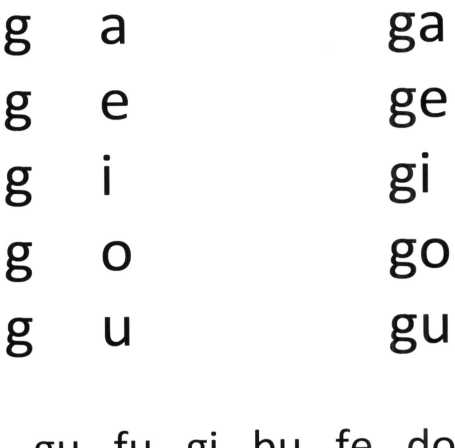

g	a		ga
g	e		ge
g	i		gi
g	o		go
g	u		gu

gu fu gi bu fe do
ba di fo du

b u bu g bug

Day 6

Uppercase E

Write an E in each box. E is just like F but you have to jump down one more time to draw a line across the bottom. Circle your best one.

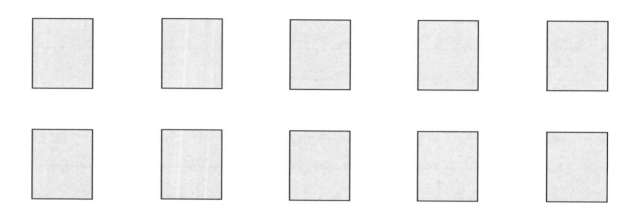

Odd Numbers

Circle pairs of footprints like the example. Every circle will have two footprints in them. Count how many footprints by skip counting by two. 2, 4,... Oh no! One foot print doesn't have a pair! That means there's an **odd** number of footprints.

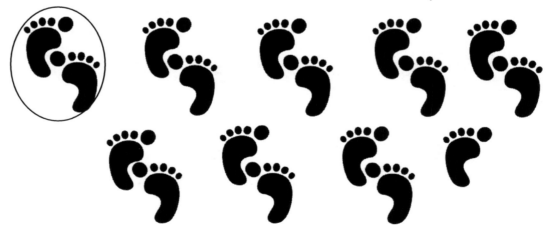

Read the consonant sound, then the short vowel sound, and then the two combined.

h	a	ha
h	e	he
h	i	hi
h	o	ho
h	u	hu

ga hu bu he da hi
fi fo ha gi ho de

h   a   ha   d   had

h   u   hu   g   hug

Day 7

Words

Count the number of boxes on the page. Touch each one and count it. There are ten. Now you are going to write three words in those ten boxes. You'll write one word on each line of boxes. Write: F E E L   I T   L I F T

Odd and Even Numbers

Which group of objects has an even number? Which group of objects has an odd number? If each object has a pair, there is an even number of objects. If one doesn't have a pair, then there is an odd number of objects.

Read the consonant sound, then the short vowel sound, and then the two combined.

j	a	ja
j	e	je
j	i	ji
j	o	jo
j	u	ju

ja   hu   fi   bu   he   da

bo   fu   ga   jo   gu   ji

j   o   jo   b   job

j   e   je   t   jet

Uppercase H

Write an H in each box. Start in the top left corner and draw a line down the side of the box. Then jump up to the other corner and draw a line down. Then jump to the middle and draw a line across. Circle your best one.

Odd and Even Numbers

Which group of objects has an even number? Which group of objects has an odd number? If each object has a pair, there is an even number of objects. If one doesn't have a pair, then there is an odd number of objects.

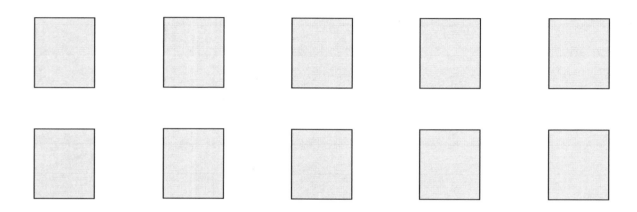

Read the consonant sound, then the short vowel sound, and then the two combined.

k	a	ka
k	e	ke
k	i	ki
k	o	ko
k	u	ku

ka	ju	fi	ku	he	di	ko
gu	da	ke	jo	bu	bo	ki

k	i	ki	d	kid

k	i	ki	t	kit

Day 9

Uppercase M

Write an M in each box. Start in the top left corner, like you did with H. Draw a line down the side of the box. Then jump up to the corner and draw a diagonal line to the bottom middle of the box. Keep going back up to the top right corner. Draw a line down the side of the box to the bottom. Circle your best one.

Odd and Even Numbers

Which set of socks has an even number? Which set of socks has an odd number? If each object has a pair, there is an even number of objects. If one doesn't have a pair, then there is an odd number of objects.

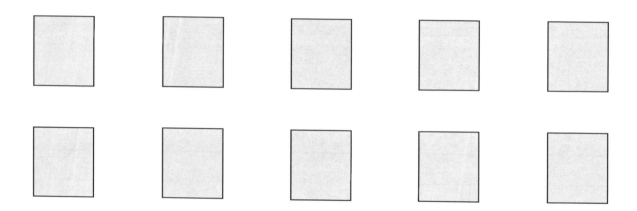

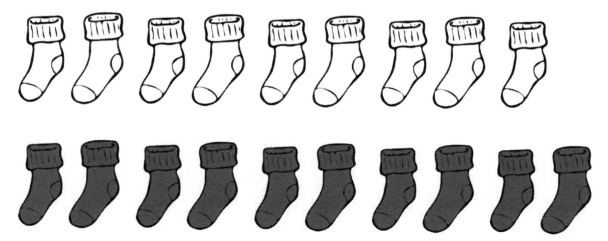

Read the consonant sound, then the short vowel sound, and then the two combined.

l	a	la
l	e	le
l	i	li
l	o	lo
l	u	lu

li	ju	fe	la	ha	lu
di	ba	le	jo	ku	lo

l	o	lo	g	log
l	e	le	g	leg
l	i	li	d	lid

Day 10

Uppercase N

Write an N in each box. Start in the top left corner. Draw a line down the side of the box to the bottom. Jump back up to the top and draw a line down to the opposite bottom corner. Then draw straight up to the top. Circle your best one.

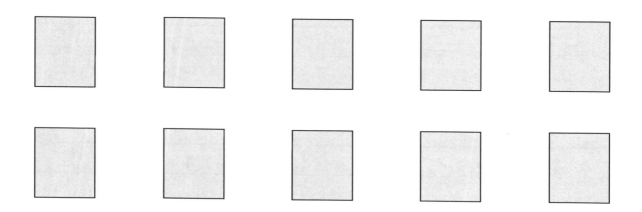

Odd and Even

Draw a line under the odd numbers, every other number, starting with 1. Draw a line above all the even numbers, every other number, starting with 2. When you're done, skip count by the odd numbers and then by the even numbers.

1 2 3 4 5 6 7 8 9 10

11 12 13 14 15 16 17 18 19 20

Read the consonant sound, then the short vowel sound, and then the two combined.

m	a	ma
m	e	me
m	i	mi
m	o	mo
m	u	mu

mu	fe	le	ma	bi	la
gu	fa	mi	jo	me	mo

m	a	ma	d	mad
m	o	mo	p	mop
m	e	me	t	met

Day 11

Uppercase V

Write a V in each box. Start in the top left corner. Draw down to the bottom middle and back up to the top right corner. Circle your best one.

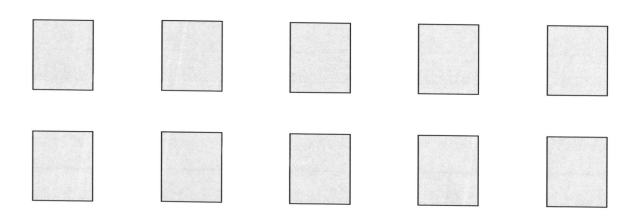

Counting by Tens

Read the numbers and words to count by tens.

10 ten
20 twenty
30 thirty
40 forty
50 fifty
60 sixty
70 seventy
80 eighty
90 ninety
100 one hundred

Read the consonant sound, then the short vowel sound, and then the two combined.

n	a	na
n	e	ne
n	i	ni
n	o	no
n	u	nu

ni   hu   de   nu   ma   bi

na   mi   jo   ne   lo   no

n	o	no	d	nod
n	e	ne	t	net
n	u	nu	t	nut

Day 12

Uppercase W

Write a W in each box. You write it like two Vs put together. Circle your best one.

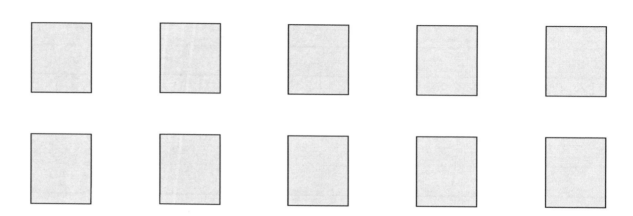

Counting by Tens

Read the numbers and words to count by tens. Then count backwards by ten starting at one hundred.

10	ten
20	twenty
30	thirty
40	forty
50	fifty
60	sixty
70	seventy
80	eighty
90	ninety
100	one hundred

Read the consonant sound, then the short vowel sound, and then the two combined.

p	a		pa
p	e		pe
p	i		pi
p	o		po
p	u		pu

na	lu	pe	nu	pi	he
fu	pa	mi	po	lo	pu

p	a	pa	n	pan
p	o	po	t	pot
p	i	pi	g	pig

Day 13

Words

Now you are going to write three words. You'll write one word on each line of boxes. Write: W I N   H I M   L I V E

Counting by Tens

What numbers are missing? Say them out loud.

10   _____   30   _____   50

60   _____   80   _____   100

Read the consonant sound, then the short vowel sound, and then the two combined.

r	a		ra
r	e		re
r	i		ri
r	o		ro
r	u		ru

ru	ge	nu	ra	ji	re
pa	ri	ho	bu	ro	fu

r	a	ra	g	rag
r	i	ri	p	rip
r	u	ru	n	run

Day 14

Uppercase X

Write an X in each box. Start in the top left corner and go down to the opposite corner at the bottom. Jump up to the top right corner and go down to the opposite bottom corner. Circle your best one.

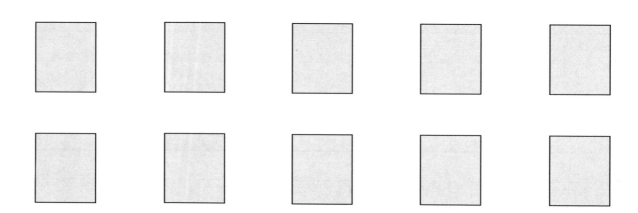

Counting by Tens

What numbers are missing? Say them out loud.

0 _____ 20 _____ 40

50 _____ 70 _____ 90

Read the consonant sound, then the short vowel sound, and then the two combined.

s	a	sa
s	e	se
s	i	si
s	o	so
s	u	su

sa	ra	mu	na	jo	fe
lu	si	hu	se	so	ki

s	a	sa	d	sad
s	i	si	t	sit
s	u	su	n	sun

Day 15

Uppercase Y

Write a Y in each box. Start in the top left and go down to the middle and back up to the top right. Jump to the bottom point of what you just wrote and draw straight down. Circle your best one.

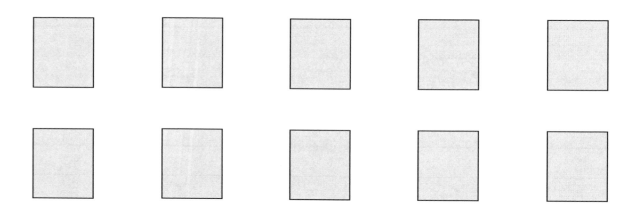

Counting 20 - 30

Read the numbers and the words to count from twenty to thirty.

20 twenty
21 twenty-one
22 twenty-two
23 twenty-three
24 twenty-four
25 twenty-five
26 twenty-six
27 twenty-seven
28 twenty-eight
29 twenty-nine
30 thirty

Read the consonant sound, then the short vowel sound, and then the two combined.

t	a	ta
t	e	te
t	i	ti
t	o	to
t	u	tu

ha	ta	le	tu	bo	je
su	na	ti	gu	to	ma

t	i	ti	p	tip
t	a	ta	g	tag
t	e	te	n	ten

Day 16

Uppercase K

Write a K in each box. Start at the top left corner. Draw a line down the side of the box. Jump up to the opposite corner at the top and draw a slanted line to the middle and then back out to the bottom corner. Circle your best one.

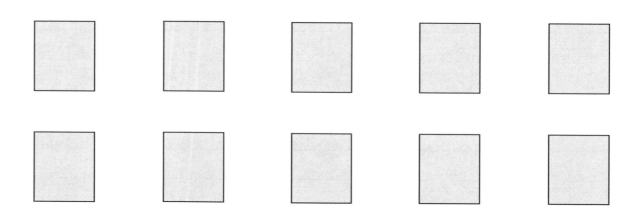

Counting to 30

Count the magnifying glasses.

Read the consonant sound, then the short vowel sound, and then the two combined.

v	a	va
v	e	ve
v	i	vi
v	o	vo
v	u	vu

va	sa	ve	tu	da	vo
tu	fa	vi	vu	ro	li

v   a   va   n   van

Day 17

Uppercase A

Write an A in each box. Start in the top middle. Draw a line down to the bottom left corner. Jump back up to the top and draw a line down to the bottom right corner. Jump up halfway and draw a line across the middle. Circle your best one.

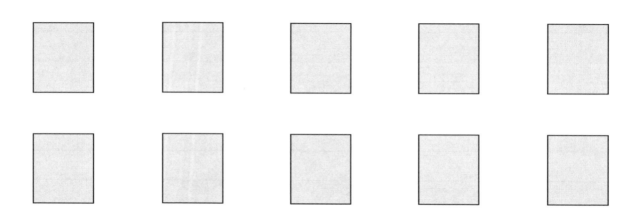

Counting by Five

How many fingers are on one hand? Count by five. Read the numbers and words to count by five.

5	five
10	ten
15	fifteen
20	twenty
25	twenty-five
30	thirty
35	thirty-five
40	forty
45	forty-five
50	fifty

Read the consonant sound, then the short vowel sound, and then the two combined.

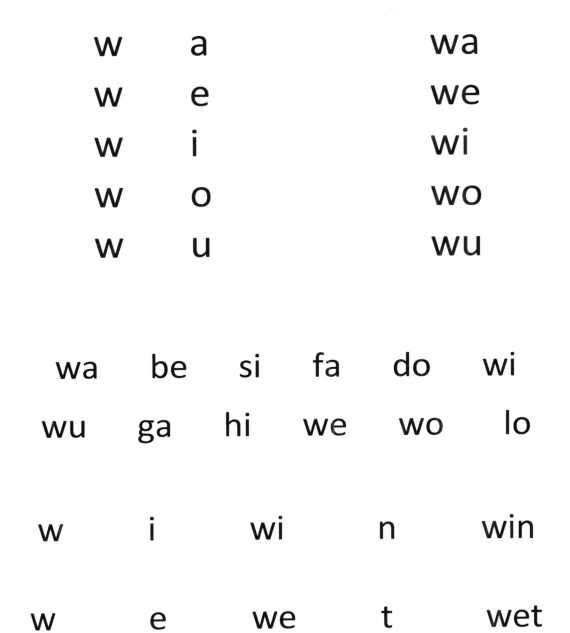

w   a   wa

w   e   we

w   i   wi

w   o   wo

w   u   wu

wa   be   si   fa   do   wi

wu   ga   hi   we   wo   lo

w   i   wi   n   win

w   e   we   t   wet

Day 18

Uppercase Z

Write a Z in each box. Start in the top left and draw across the top of the box to the top right corner. Then draw down to the bottom left corner of the box and then across the bottom of the box to the other corner. Circle your best one.

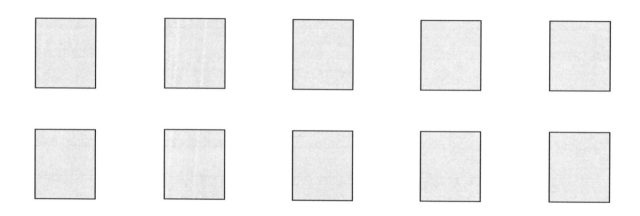

Counting by Five

Count the fingers by counting by five.

| 5 |
| 10 |
| 15 |
| 20 |
| 25 |
| 30 |
| 35 |

Read the consonant sound, then the short vowel sound, and then the two combined.

y	a	ya
y	e	ye
y	i	yi
y	o	yo
y	u	yu

yi	ga	de	ni	ra	yu	to
mu	ya	li	ye	vu	yo	ki

y   a   ya   p   yap

Day 19

Words

Now you are going to write three words. You'll write one word on each line of boxes. Write: F I X   K A Y   K I T E

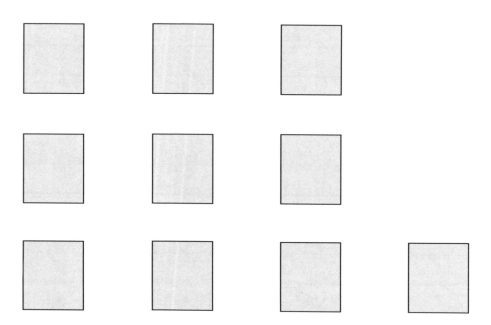

Counting by Five

Count the fingers by counting by five.

Read the consonant sound, then the short vowel sound, and then the two combined.

z	a	za
z	e	ze
z	i	zi
z	o	zo
z	u	zu

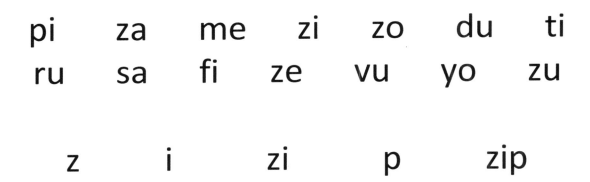

pi   za   me   zi   zo   du   ti

ru   sa   fi   ze   vu   yo   zu

z   i   zi   p   zip

Uppercase O and Q

Write an O in each box. Start at the top and draw a circle. Circle your best one. Then add a tail to each to turn them into Qs.

Odd and Even Numbers

Which set of socks has an even number? Which set of socks has an odd number? If each object has a pair, there is an even number of objects. If one doesn't have a pair, then there is an odd number of objects.

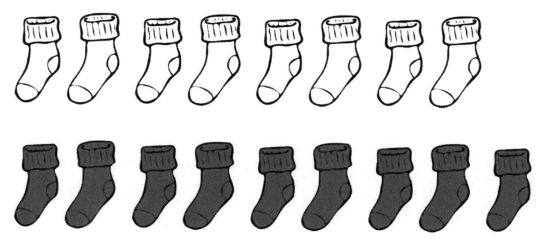

Read across the lines. Start with the two individual sounds, then two sounds combined, and then those same two letters together with different ending sounds added on.

b a   ba   bad   bag   bam   bat

b e   be   bed   beg   Ben   bell
bet

b i   bi   bid   big   bin   bit   biz

b o   bo   bob   bog   bop

b u   bu   bud   bug   bun   bum
bus   but   buzz

dog   the   ran

The dog.

The dog ran.

Day 21

Uppercase C

Write a C in each box. C is like part of an O. Circle your best one.

Counting by Fives

What numbers are missing? Say them out loud.

5   _____   15   _____   25

30   _____   40   _____   50

Read across the lines. Start with the two individual sounds, then two sounds combined, and then those same two letters together with different ending sounds added on.

d　a　da　　dab　dad　dam

d　e　de　　den

d　i　di　　did　dig　dim　dip

d　o　do　　dog　dop　dot

d　u　du　　dub　dud　dug

cat　　　mat　　　is　　　on

The cat.　　The mat.

Is the cat on the mat?

The cat is on the mat.

Day 22

Uppercase G

Write a G in each box. G is like a C with a little shelf drawn on top of the end. Circle your best one.

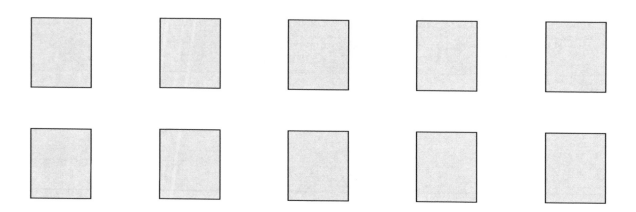

Counting by Fives

What numbers are missing? Say them out loud.

0   _____   10   _____   20

25   _____   35   _____   45

Read across the lines. Start with the two individual sounds, then two sounds combined, and then those same two letters together with different ending sounds added on.

f a   fa   fab   fad   fan   fat

f e   fe   fed   fell

f i   fi   fib   fig   fill   fin

         fit   fizz

f o   fo   fog

f u   fu   fun   fuzz

it his pen hand a has man in

The man.   A pen.

The man has a pen.

Is the pen in his hand?

It is in his hand.

Day 23

Uppercase U

Write a U in each box. Start in the top middle. Start at the top and curve down and back up. Make sure you touch the bottom of the box and go all the way back up to the top of the box. Circle your best one.

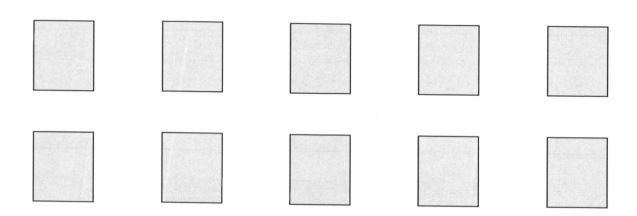

Counting by Twos

What even numbers are missing? Say them out loud. Hint: skip by two.

6 _____ 10 _____ 14

16 _____ 20 _____ 24

Read across the lines. Start with the two individual sounds, then two sounds combined, and then those same two letters together with different ending sounds added on.

g a   ga   gab   gag   gal   gap

g e   ge   get

g i   gi   gill

g o   go   gob   God   got

g u   gu   gun   gut

big   hen   fat   rat   box   run   from   can

A fat hen.   A big rat.

The fat hen is on the box.

The rat ran from the box.

Can the hen run?

Day 24

Uppercase J

Write a J in each box. Start in the top middle and draw down and then curve to the edge of the box. Draw a line across the top of the box. Circle your best one.

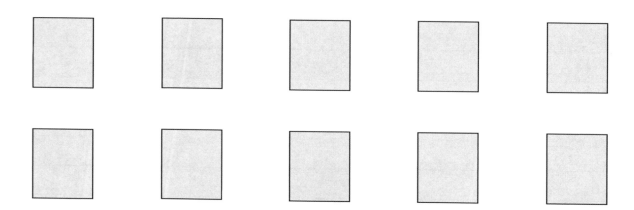

Counting by Twos

What odd numbers are missing? Say them out loud. Hint: skip count by two.

5   _____   9   _____   13

17   _____   21   _____   25

Read across the lines. Start with the two individual sounds, then two sounds combined, and then those same two letters together with different ending sounds added on.

h a   ha   had   ham   hat

h e   he   hen   hell

h i   hi   hid   hill   him   hit

h o   ho   hog   hop   hot

h u   hu   hug   hut

Spot   Anna   hat   catch   see

See Spot!   See Anna!

See!   Spot has the hat.

Can Anna catch Spot?

Day 25

Words

Now you are going to write three words. You'll write one word on each line of boxes. Write: J U G   F O X   C A K E

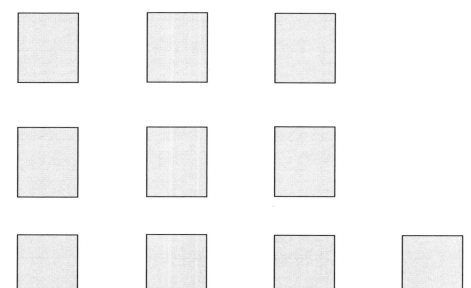

Counting 30 - 40

Read the numbers and the words to count from thirty to forty.

30   thirty
31   thirty-one
32   thirty-two
33   thirty-three
34   thirty-four
35   thirty-five
36   thirty-six
37   thirty-seven
38   thirty-eight
39   thirty-nine
40   forty

Read across the lines. Start with the two individual sounds, then two sounds combined, and then those same two letters together with different ending sounds added on.

l a   la   lab   lad   lag   lap

l e   le   led   leg   let   less

l i   li   lid   lip   lit

l o   lo   log   lop   lot

l u   lu   lug

she   pat   too   now   let   me

Anna can catch Spot.

See! She has the hat.

Now Anna can pat Spot.

Let me pat Spot, too.

Day 26

Uppercase S

Write an S in each box. Start on the top right of the box and curve your way down to the bottom left of the box. Make sure you touch the top and bottom of the box. Circle your best one.

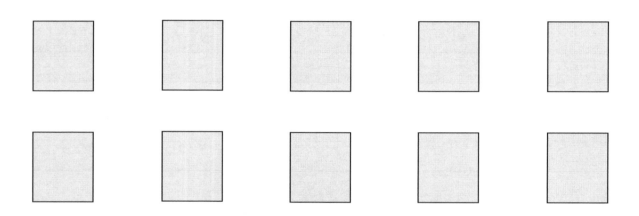

Counting Objects

Count the number of cars.

Read across the lines. Start with the two individual sounds, then two sounds combined, and then those same two letters together with different ending sounds added on.

m a   ma   mad   man   map   mat

m e   me   men   met

m i   mi   mid   mill   miss

m o   mo   mob   mom   mop

m u   mu   mud   mug   mutt

Ned   eggs   left   fed   nest
them   get   will   black   hen

Ned has fed the hen. She is a black hen. She has left the nest.

See the eggs in the nest!

Will the hen let Ned get them?

Uppercase D

Write a D in each box. Start in the top left corner. Draw a line down the side of the box to the bottom of the box. Jump back up to the top. Draw a curve down to the bottom corner so that it meets your first line. Circle your best one.

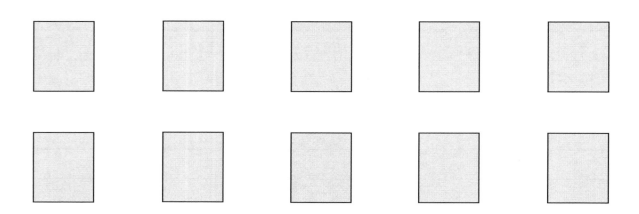

Counting 40 - 50

Read the numbers and the words to count from forty to fifty.

40   forty
41   forty-one
42   forty-two
43   forty-three
44   forty-four
45   forty-five
46   forty-six
47   forty-seven
48   forty-eight
49   forty-nine
50   fifty

Read across the lines. Start with the two individual sounds, then two sounds combined, and then those same two letters together with different ending sounds added on.

n a   na   nab   nag   nap

n e   ne   Ned   net

n i   ni   nip

n o   no   nod   not

n u   nu   nut

head   he   Matt   come   with   and

Let me get the black hat.

Now Ned has it on his head, and he is a big man.

Come, Matt, see the big man with his black hat.

Day 28

Uppercase P

Write a P in each box. Start in the top left corner. Draw a line down the left side of the box. Jump back up to the top and draw a curve back to the middle of the line. Circle your best one.

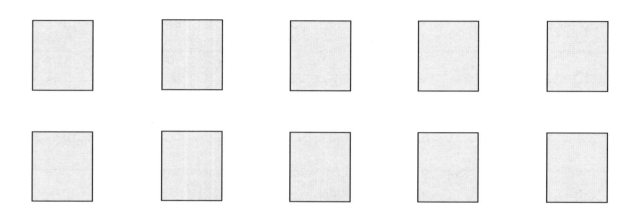

Counting by Five

Count the fingers by counting by five. 5, 10, 15, 20, 25, 30, 35, ...

Read across the lines. Start with the two individual sounds, then two sounds combined, and then those same two letters together with different ending sounds added on.

p a   pa   pad   pan   pal   pat

p e   pe   peg   pen   pep   pet

p i   pi   pig   pill   pin   pit

p o   po   pod   pop   pot

p u   pu   pub   pun   pup

Ned is on the box. He has a pen in his hand. A big rat is in the box. Can the dog catch the rat?

Come with me, Anna, and see the man with a black hat on his head.

The fat hen has left the nest. Run, Matt, and get the eggs.

Day 29

Uppercase R

Write an R in each box. Draw a P and then add a leg. Circle your best one.

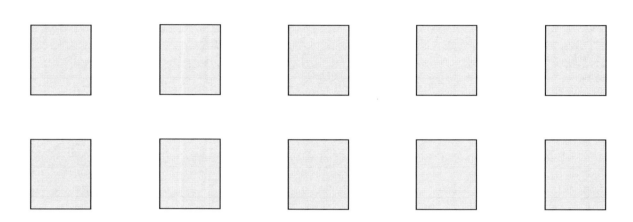

Counting Objects

Count the number of pens.

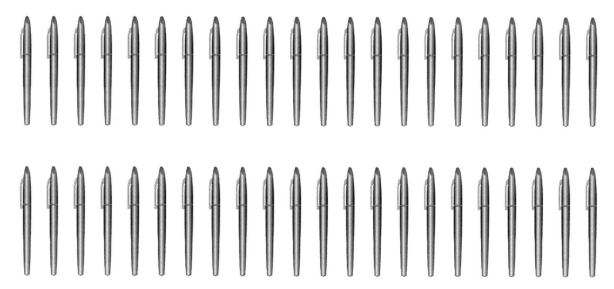

Read across the lines. Start with the two individual sounds, then two sounds combined, and then those same two letters together with different ending sounds added on.

r a   ra   rad   rag   ran   rat

r e   re   red

r i   ri   rib   rid   rim   rip

r o   ro   rob   rod   rot

r u   ru   rub   rug   run   rut

Emma   some   pan   him   yes   do   you   have   to

Do you see Emma?

Yes; she has a pan with some eggs in it.

Let me have the pan and the eggs, will you, Emma?

Has the black hen left the nest?

I will now run to catch Spot. Will you run, too?

Day 30

Uppercase B

Write a B in each box. Draw a P and then add a belly. Circle your best one.

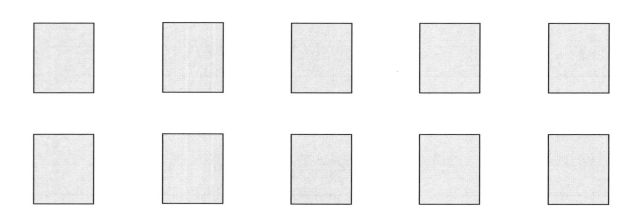

Counting Forward and Backward

Count to ten forward and backward. Then count to one hundred by tens forward and backward. You can do it!

They are cheering for you!

Read across the lines. Start with the two individual sounds, then two sounds combined, and then those same two letters together with different ending sounds added on.

s a   sa   sad   sag   sap   sat

s e   se   sell   set

s i   si   sin   sip   sit

s o   so   sob   sop

s u   su   sub   sun   sum   sup

Oh   whip   Ben   up   still   sit   if   stand   Jim

Oh Ben! Let me get in, will you?

Yes, if you will sit still.

Stand still, Jim, and let Anna get in.

Now, Ben, hand me the whip.

Get up, Jim!

Day 31

Words

Now you are going to write three words. You'll write one word on each line of boxes. Write: P A D S   B R I C K S

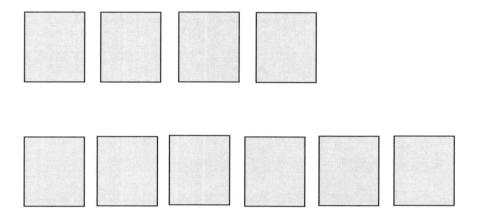

Counting 50 - 60

Read the numbers and the words to count from fifty to sixty.

50   fifty
51   fifty-one
52   fifty-two
53   fifty-three
54   fifty-four
55   fifty-five
56   fifty-six
57   fifty-seven
58   fifty-eight
59   fifty-nine
60   sixty

Read across the lines. Start with the two individual sounds, then two sounds combined, and then those same two letters together with different ending sounds added on.

t a   ta   tab   tad   tag   tan   tap

t e   te   Ted   tell   ten

t i   ti   tin   tip

t o   to   tot

t u   tu   tub   tug

Katy   nice   sweet   sing   just   hang

cage   then   song   pet   put   not

Katy has a nice pet. It can sing a sweet song. She has just fed it. She will now put it in the cage, and hang the cage up. Then the cat cannot catch it.

Day 32

Your Name

Ask a parent or older sibling to write your name in the row of blocks. Now you write your name in the other rows. **Use all CAPS.**

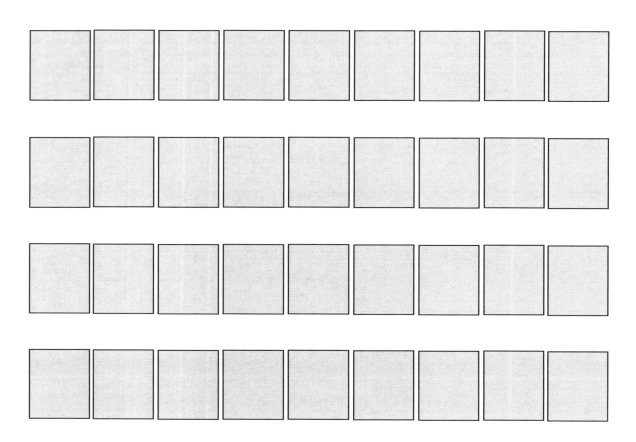

Counting

Count by tens to one hundred. Count by fives to one hundred. Then can you count backward from ten and from one hundred by tens?

They are applauding you!

Vv

van   vet

Ww

wag   wet   win

Yy

yap   yet

Zz

zig   zag   zap

-ad   bad had lad mad pad sad

-an   ban can Dan fan pan ran

-at   bat cat fat hat mat pat sat

-en   Ben den hen men pen ten

Lowercase C

In the block, write a big letter C. Next to it write a whole row of little c. On your sheet the block goes up high for the big, or capital C. When you write your little c, it will only go between the two lines on the paper. The top of the little c will touch the top line and the bottom of the little c will touch the bottom line. Circle your best one.

Counting by Fives

What numbers are missing? Say them out loud.

25 _____ 35 _____ 45

50 _____ 60 _____ 70

Rhyming Words

First figure out the underlined sound. Then add on the different first sounds to make words. Each row starts with the letter B. It's okay to point out the Bs to make sure they aren't confusing them with Ds.

b<u>et</u>	get	met	jet	pet	set
b<u>id</u>	did	hid	lid	kid	rid
b<u>in</u>	fin	pin	sin	tin	
b<u>it</u>	fit	hit	pit	sit	wit
b<u>op</u>	cop	hop	lop	top	mop
b<u>ot</u>	got	hot	lot	pot	not
b<u>un</u>	fun	gun	pun	run	sun
b<u>ut</u>	cut	gut	hut	nut	rut

Day 34

Lowercase A

In the block on your page, write a big letter A. Next to it write a whole row of little a. It starts like a c, and then has one more line. Draw a little c and then jump to the top line and draw a side line down to make the a. Circle the best one.

Counting by Fives and Tens

Count the stacks of coins by fives and then by tens by putting them in pairs. There are five coins in each stack of coins.

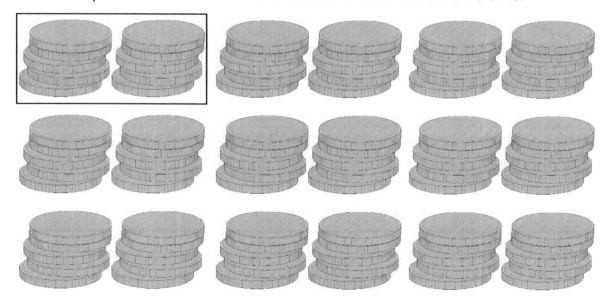

Word Pairs

Start on the left and sound out the words. The second pair of words rhyme with the first set. When words end with the same letters, they usually rhyme.

bad lid	had kid
mad Dan	sad man
ban sin	can pin
fan men	ran ten
bat top	cat mop
fat pet	hat wet
hot mat	got rat

Day 35

Lowercase D

In the block write a big letter D. Next to it write a whole row of little d. To write d you start by writing a little c, then you jump up above the top line and draw a line down. It's like an a but with an arm reaching up. Circle the best one.

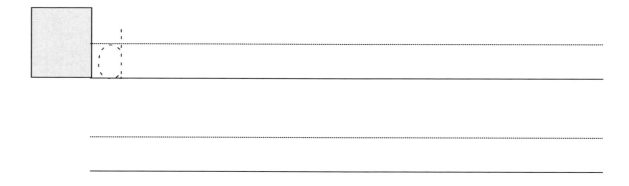

Counting 60 - 70

Read the numbers and the words to count from sixty to seventy.

60 sixty
61 sixty-one
62 sixty-two
63 sixty-three
64 sixty-four
65 sixty-five
66 sixty-six
67 sixty-seven
68 sixty-eight
69 sixty-nine
70 seventy

Tom   top   Katy's   at   back

look   good   doll   think   spot

Look at Tom and his dog. The dog has a black spot on his back. Do you think he is a good dog?

Tom has a big top, too. It is on the box with Katy's doll.

ten men	hot pot	rat sat
hid rot	get pen	met tot
kid hop	pet cat	hid top
did run	cut lid	hot sun

Day 36

Writing Words

Write the words: add, cad, add. Put your finger down to make a space between each word.

Counting Objects

Count the circles.

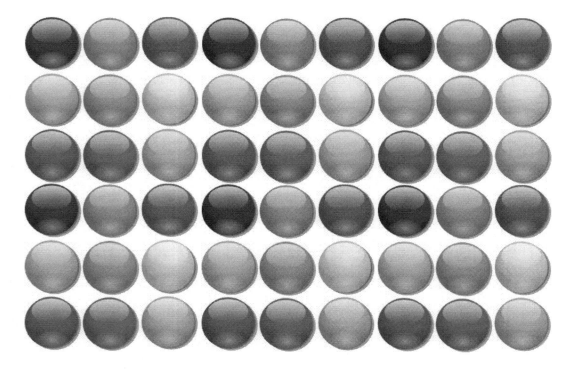

Sentences

Practice with these word pairs and then build sentences. The words repeat, so don't worry about the sentences getting longer.

hid nut   hot lid   men run   got mop

I met a dog.
I met a fun dog.
I met a fun, fat dog.
I met a fun, fat, wet dog.
I met Sam, a fun, fat, wet dog.

I fed a cat.
I fed a hot cat.
I fed a hot, mad cat.
I fed a hot, mad cat a bit.

I can sit.
I can sit and hop.
I can sit, hop and run.
I can sit, hop, run and jog.

Day 37

Lowercase G

In the block on your page, write a big letter G. Next to it write a whole row of little g. To write a g, you will start with writing a little c. You then close the c like you are writing an a, *but* you keep going and give it a tail. Circle your best one.

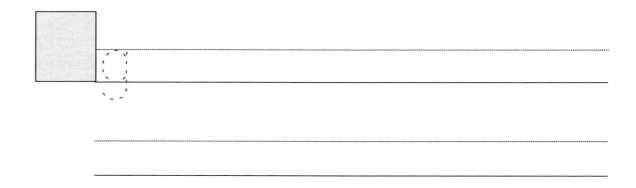

What numbers are missing?

Read the numbers out loud and fill in the missing numbers as you read.

47   48   49   _____   51   52   _____   54   55   56

57   _____   59   60   _____   62   63   _____   65

66   _____   68   _____   70   71   _____   73   74

75   _____   77   78   79   _____   81   82   83   _____

Hard C-K Sound

The letter C makes the S sound when it is followed by an E or an I, so here the K is substituted in for those vowels to practice the CK sound.

c a	ca	cap	cat	can
k e	ke	Ken	keg	
k i	ki	kid	kit	kiss
c o	co	cod	cop	cot
c u	cu	cup	cut	cub

sun we how pond stop for go
swim her us hot duck

The sun is up. The man has fed the black hen and the fat duck. Now the duck will swim in the pond. The hen has run to her nest.

Day 38

Lowercase O

In the block on your page, write a big letter O. Next to it write a whole row of little o. Circle your best one.

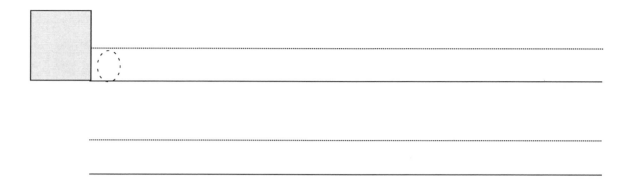

Counting to and from 20

Use the number line to count up to 20. Touch each number as you say it. One, two, ... Then count backwards from 20 using the number line. 20, 19, ...

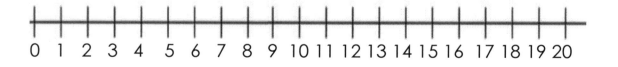

C, K

cut cap   can cut   kiss Ken
cop cup   cat cot   cod kit

John   rock   set   jump   fun   must   may

under   skip   bank   but   touch

Oh John! the sun has just set. It is not hot, now. Let us run and jump. I think it is fun to run, and skip, and jump.

See the duck on the pond! Her nest is up on the bank, under the rock. We must not touch the nest, but we may look at it.

Lowercase B

In the block on your page, write a big letter B. Next to it write a whole row of little b. The letter b has an arm that reaches up over the top line. Circle your best one.

Counting Objects

Get out something in your house you can find a lot of: paper clips, coins, etc. Spill them out and then put them away one at a time, counting each one as you go. How many are there?

She's cheering for you!

CK End Sound

CK together just make one "K" sound. Read across the rows. If that's proving too hard, you can use the rhymes and read down the columns in the first section.

pack	deck	sick	sock	buck
rack	peck	tick	rock	duck
sack	neck	pick	tock	muck
back	deck	lick	lock	luck

Review

The sun has set, and the pond is still.

John, Ned, Ben, Tom, and Emma stand on the bank, and look at the duck.

(You can stop here if that's enough for today. We'll have this reading for three days. You can read the rest to your child.)

The dog with a black spot on his back, is with Tom. See! Tom has his hat in his hand. He has left his big top on the box.

Katy's doll is on the rock.

Emma has put her pet in the cage. It will sing a sweet song. The duck has her nest under the rock.

It is not hot now. Let us run, and skip, and jump on the bank. Do you not think it is fun?

Day 40

Writing Words

Write the words: bog, bad, good. Put your finger down to make a space between each word.

Counting 70 - 80

Read the numbers and the words to count from seventy to eighty.

70   seventy
71   seventy-one
72   seventy-two
73   seventy-three
74   seventy-four
75   seventy-five
76   seventy-six
77   seventy-seven
78   seventy-eight
79   seventy-nine
80   eighty

CK

kiss cat
pick lock
lick cup
sock sack
rock kit
neck cut

Review

(You could read the beginning together simultaneously up to where you left off.*)

The sun has set, and the pond is still.

John, Ned, Ben, Tom, and Emma stand on the bank, and look at the duck.*

The dog with a black spot on his back, is with Tom. See! Tom has his hat in his hand. He has left his big top on the box.

Katy's doll is on the rock.

(You can stop here if that's enough for today. We'll have this reading one more day.)

Emma has put her pet in the cage. It will sing a sweet song. The duck has her nest under the rock.

It is not hot now. Let us run, and skip, and jump on the bank. Do you not think it is fun?

Lowercase P

In the block on your page, write a big letter P. Next to it write a whole row of little p. Little p is one of the letters with a tail that goes down below the line. Circle your best one.

Shapes

Draw a circle and an oval. What's the difference?

CK

| back pack | hot deck | fed duck |
| tick tock | pack hat | hot rock |

Review

(You could read the beginning together simultaneously up to where you left off. *)

The sun has set, and the pond is still.

John, Ned, Ben, Tom, and Emma stand on the bank, and look at the duck.

The dog with a black spot on his back, is with Tom. See! Tom has his hat in his hand. He has left his big top on the box.

Katy's doll is on the rock.

Emma has put her pet in the cage. It will sing a sweet song. The duck has her nest under the rock. *

It is not hot now. Let us run, and skip, and jump on the bank. Do you not think it is fun?

Lowercase Q

In the block on your page, write a big letter Q. Next to it write a whole row of little q. Little q is one of the letters with a tail that goes down below the line. Circle your best one.

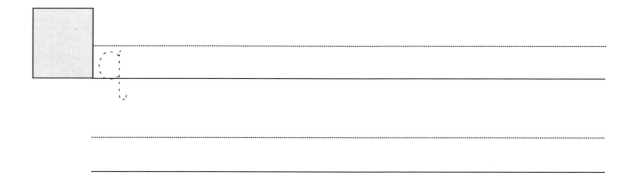

Counting 80 - 90

Read the numbers and the words to count from eighty to ninety.

80 eighty
81 eighty-one
82 eighty-two
83 eighty-three
84 eighty-four
85 eighty-five
86 eighty-six
87 eighty-seven
88 eighty-eight
89 eighty-nine
90 ninety

ND

and	sand
band	hand
land	sand and land

Kate   old   no   grass   dear   likes   be

drink   milk   cow   out   gives

Oh Kate! The old cow is in the pond: see her drink! Will she not come out to get some grass?

No, John, she likes to be in the pond. See how still she stands!

The dear old cow gives us sweet milk to drink.

Day 43

Lowercase E

In the block on your page, write a big letter E. Next to it write a whole row of little e. Little e starts in the middle and circles up to touch the top line and down to touch the bottom line. If you are unsure, ask someone to show you how to write it. Circle your best one.

Shapes

Draw a square and a rectangle. What's the difference?

ND

end   bend

fend   mend

tend   tend and mend

mama   large   as   papa   arms   ride

far   barn   both   Prince   trot   your

Papa, will you let me ride with you on Prince? I will sit still in your arms.

See, mama! We are both on Prince. How large he is!

Get up, Prince! You are not too fat to trot as far as the barn.

Writing Words

Write the words: peg, bed, goop. Put your finger down to make a space between each word.

Counting from 90 - 100

Read the numbers and the words to count from ninety to one hundred.

90	ninety
91	ninety-one
92	ninety-two
93	ninety-three
94	ninety-four
95	ninety-five
96	ninety-six
97	ninety-seven
98	ninety-eight
99	ninety-nine
100	one hundred

pond   pond end
fun fund   fund and fend

I am at a big pond.

of   that   toss   fall   well   Tammy

ball   wall   was   pretty   done   what

O Tammy, what a pretty ball!

Yes; can you catch it, Anna?

Toss it to me, and see. I will not let it fall.

That was well done.

Now, Tammy, toss it to the top of the wall, if you can.

Day 45

Lowercase L

In the block on your page, write a big letter L. Next to it write a whole row of little l. Little l is one of the letters that reaches up above the top line. Circle your best one.

Shapes

Draw a triangle and a diamond. What's the difference?

ST

-ast	fast	last
	mast	past

-est	best	nest
	pest	rest

-ist	fist	list

-ust	just	must

Day 46

Lowercase T

In the block on your page, write a big letter T. Next to it write a whole row of little t. Little t is another one of the letters that reaches up above the top line. Circle your best one.

Reading Numbers to 100

Read these numbers.

4	17	11	25	33	48
12	50	9	71	62	86
90	20	15	47	59	19
21	28	30	91	83	74
39	65	70	48	24	52

You won a ribbon for your great effort!

had   went   call   might   flag

near   swam   swing

Did you call us, mama? I went with Tom to the pond. I had my doll, and Tom had his flag.

The fat duck swam to the bank, and we fed her. Did you think we might fall into the pond?

We did not go too near, did we, Tom?

May we go to the swing, now, mama?

Day 47

Lowercase H

In the block on your page, write a big letter H. Next to it write a whole row of little h. Little h is one of the letters that reaches up above the line. Circle your best one.

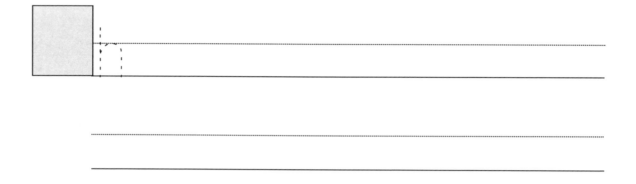

Counting Backward

Count backward from 100! You could move your finger along these number lists to keep track of where you are.

10	1
20	2
30	3
40	4
50	5
60	6
70	7
80	8
90	9
100	10

FT

raft   left   soft

gift   lift   loft

sift   tuft

here band hear horse play they should

pass where front fine hope comes

Here comes the band! Should we call mama and Tammy to see it? Let us stand still, and hear the men play as they pass.

I hope they will stop here and play for us. See the large man in front of the band, with his big hat.

(to be continued…)

Day 48

Writing Words

Write the words: hat, hot, bell. Put your finger down to make a space between each word.

Adding with Objects

What's three plus two? Count the hamsters to find out.

$+$

3 + 2 = 5

Three plus two equals five.

MP

camp	damp
lamp	ramp
limp	romp
bump	jump
pump	rump

Finish the story. *Shows where you left off.

here   band   hear   horse   play   they   should

pass   where   front   fine   hope   comes

Here comes the band! Should we call mama and Tammy to see it? Let us stand still, and hear the men play as they pass.

I hope they will stop here and play for us. See the large man in front of the band, with his big hat.* What has he in his hand? How fine he looks!

Look, too, at the man on that fine horse. If the men do not stop, let us go with them and see where they go.

Day 49

Lowercase K

In the block on your page, write a big letter K. Next to it write a whole row of little k. Little k is one of the letters that reaches up above the line. Circle your best one.

Adding with Objects

What's two plus five? Count the motorcycles to find out.

$2 + 5 = 7$

Two plus five equals seven.

MP

gift <u>lamp</u>   lift ramp   left camp

damp raft   <u>bump</u> nest   jump fast

Jump in the pond.

Olive   happy   make   cart   tent   woods

little   very   bed   Robert   gone   draw

Olive and Robert are very happy; papa and mama have gone to the woods with them. Robert has a big tent and a flag, and Olive has a little bed for her doll.

Day 50

Lowercase I

In the block on your page, write a big letter I. Next to it write a whole row of little i. To write little i you start on the top line and draw straight down. Then you jump up and put the dot above the line. Circle your best one.

Adding with Objects

What's four plus four? Count the bicycles to find out.

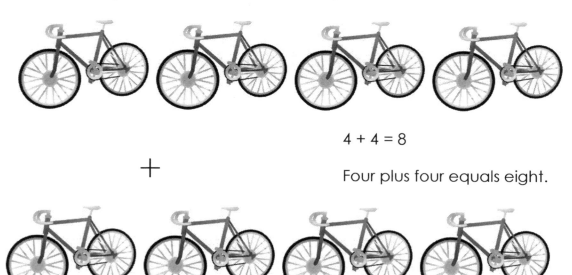

4 + 4 = 8

Four plus four equals eight.

NT

Look for repeating letter patterns and practice them. Read down these lists to make it easier or across for a challenge.

w<u>ent</u>	tent	r<u>un</u>t
bent	m<u>int</u>	hunt
rent	tint	punt
sent	lint	pant

Finish the story. *Shows where you left off.

Olive   happy   make   cart   tent   woods

little   very   bed   Robert   gone   draw

Olive and Robert are very happy; papa and mama have gone to the woods with them. Robert has a big tent and a flag, and Olive has a little bed for her doll.*

Jim is with them.

Robert will make him draw Olive and her doll in the cart.

Day 51

Lowercase J

In the block on your page, write a big letter J. Next to it write a whole row of little j. Little j is one of the letters that has a tail under the bottom line. Circle your best one.

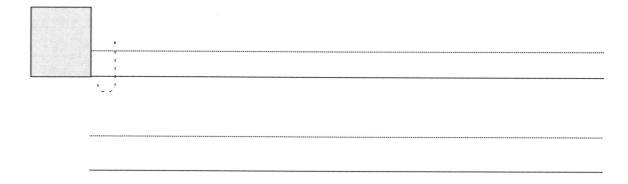

Subtracting with Objects

What's six minus two? Count the stuffed animals to find out. How many are there all together? Two are crossed off. They were given away. How many are left?

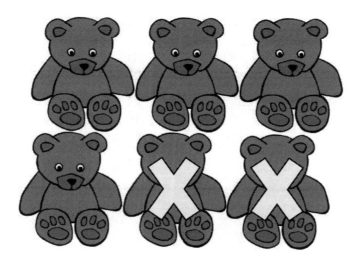

6 - 2 = 4
Six minus two four equals four.

LT

belt   felt   melt   pelt
hilt   kilt   tilt   wilt

James Mary made sang my lay Kate

spade lap dig doll's sand said

"Kate, will you play with me?" said James. "We will dig in the sand with this little spade. That will be fun."

"Not now James" said Kate; "for I must make my doll's bed. Get Mary to play with you."

Day 52

Writing Words

Write the words: jig, kid, kite. Put your finger down to make a space between each word.

_____

_____

Subtracting with Objects

What's five minus three? Count the cows to find out. How many are there all together? Three are crossed off. They went away. How many are left?

5 – 3 = 2   Five minus three equals two.

Finish the story. *Shows where you left off.

James   Mary   made   sang   my   lay   Kate

spade   lap   dig   doll's   sand   said

"Kate, will you play with me?" said James. "We will dig in the sand with this little spade. That will be fun."

"Not now James" said Kate; "for I must make my doll's bed. Get Mary to play with you."*

James went to get Mary to play with him. Then Kate made the doll's bed.

She sang a song to her doll, and the doll lay very still in her lap.

Did the doll hear Kate sing?

Day 53

Lowercase F

In the block on your page, write a big letter F. Next to it write a whole row of little f. Little f is one of the letters that reaches up above the line. Circle your best one.

Subtracting with Objects

What's four minus two? Count the dolphins to find out. How many are there all together? Three are crossed off. They went hunting for fish. How many are left?

4 − 2 = 2   Four minus two equals two.

Review

sent felt   melt mint   pant belt

hunt pelt   tilt tent   last sand

The duck is a runt.

I went and felt the sand.

He went up the ramp fast.

Last on the list is the lamp. It is at the end.

Day 54

Lowercase N

In the block on your page, write a big letter N. Next to it write a whole row of little n. Circle your best one.

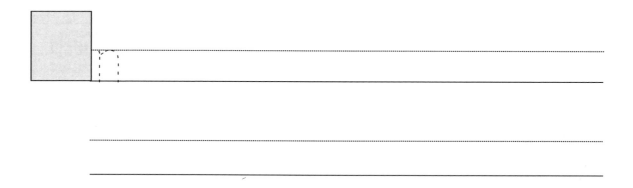

Counting by Fives

What numbers are missing? Say them out loud.

50   _____   60   _____   70

75   _____   85   _____   95

LK

milk   silk   bulk
hulk   sulk

its   shade   brook   picks   all
by   help   stones   glad   soft

Kate has left her doll in its little bed, and has gone to play with Mary and James. They are all in the shade, now, by the brook.

James digs in the soft sand with his spade.

Lowercase M

In the block on your page, write a big letter M. Next to it write a whole row of little m. Little m starts like n but has an extra bump. Circle your best one.

Counting by Twos

What odd numbers are missing? Say them out loud.

55 _____ 59 _____ 63

13 _____ 17 _____ 21

LD

held meld weld

its   shade   brook   picks   all
by   help   stones   glad   soft

(You could read the beginning together simultaneously up to where you left off.*)

Kate has left her doll in its little bed, and has gone to play with Mary and James. They are all in the shade, now, by the brook.

James digs in the soft sand with his spade,* and Mary picks up little stones and puts them in her lap.

James and Mary are glad to see Kate. She will help them pick up stones and dig, by the little brook.

Day 56

Writing Words

Write the words: flap, men, ninja. Put your finger down to make a space between each word.

....

_____

....

_____

Counting by Twos

What even numbers are missing? Say them out loud.

62   _____   66   _____   70

80   _____   84   _____   88

Blending Sounds

held milk   silk pant   gift list

I just held the soft silk.

The list had milk.

Review

"What should we do?" said Tammy to John. "I do not like to sit still. Should we hunt for eggs in the barn?"

"No," said John; "I like to play on the grass."

Day 57

Lowercase R

In the block on your page, write a big letter R. Next to it write a whole row of little r. Circle your best one.

Counting by Tens

Count the number of toe prints by counting by tens. 10, 20, ...
Then can you count down by tens? 100, 90, ...

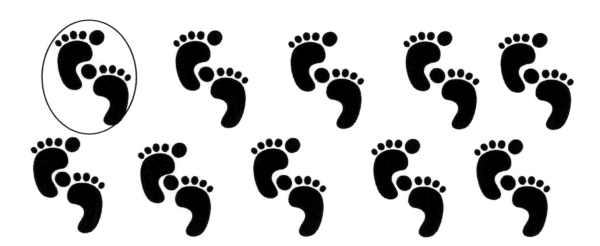

LF

elf   self   gulf

Review
(You could read the beginning together simultaneously up to where you left off.*)

"What should we do?" said Tammy to John. "I do not like to sit still. Should we hunt for eggs in the barn?"

"No," said John; "I like to play on the grass.* Will not papa let us catch Prince, and go to the big woods?"

"We can put the tent in the cart and go to some nice spot where the grass is soft and sweet."

Day 58

Lowercase S

In the block on your page, write a big letter S. Next to it write a whole row of little s. Circle your best one.

Counting by Fives and Tens

Count the stacks of coins by fives. There are five coins in each stack of coins.

LP

help   kelp

gulp   pulp

Review
(You could read the beginning together simultaneously up to where you left off.*)

"What should we do?" said Tammy to John. "I do not like to sit still. Should we hunt for eggs in the barn?"

"No," said John; "I like to play on the grass. Will not papa let us catch Prince and go to the big woods?"

"We can put the tent in the cart and go to some nice spot where the grass is soft and sweet."*

"That will be fine," said Tammy. "I will get my doll and give her a ride with us."

"Yes," said John, "and we will get mama to go, too. She will hang up a swing for us in the shade."

Day 59

Lowercase U

In the block on your page, write a big letter U. Next to it write a whole row of little u. Circle your best one.

Counting Objects

Count the bats.

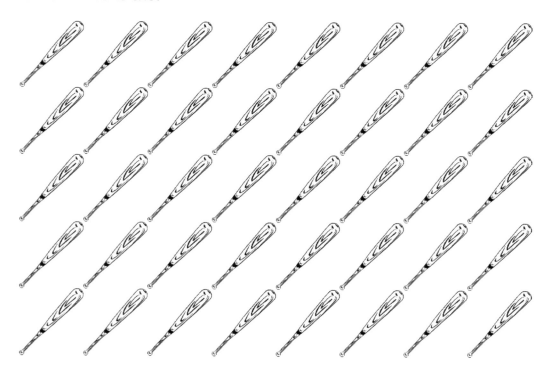

PT

kept   wept

peep   while   take   sleep   tuck   safe   oh

wet   feet   chick   can't   feels   wing

Peep, peep! Where have you gone, little chick? Are you lost? Can't you get back to the hen?

Oh, here you are! I will take you back. Here, hen, take this little chick under your wing.

Now, chick, tuck your little, wet feet under you, and go to sleep for a while.

Peep, peep! How safe the little chick feels now!

Day 60

Writing Words

Write the words: runs, slurp, turn. Put your finger down to make a space between each word.

Adding and Subtracting with Objects

Draw objects and then write the math equation it shows.

Blending Sounds

kept golf   kelp gulf
self help   pump pulp

The elf wept in the tent.

wind   time   there   fence   kite   high
eyes   bright   flies   why   day   shines

This is a fine day. The sun shines bright. There is a good wind, and my kite flies high. I can just see it.

The sun shines in my eyes; I will stand in the shade of this high fence.

Day 61

Lowercase V

In the block on your page, write a big letter V. Next to it write a whole row of little v. Circle your best one.

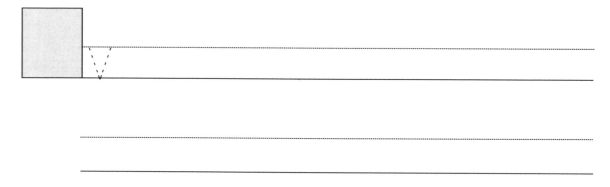

Adding with Objects

What is seven plus six? Draw seven lines and six circles (unless you really want to draw something else). Then count them all up. How many are there all together?

7 + 6 = ?

SK

bask   mask   task

desk   risk   disk

tusk

Finish the story.

wind   time   there   fence   kite   high

eyes   bright   flies   why   day   shines

This is a fine day. The sun shines bright. There is a good wind, and my kite flies high. I can just see it.

The sun shines in my eyes; I will stand in the shade of this high fence.

Why, here comes my dog! He was under the cart. Did you see him there?

What a good time we had! Are you glad that we did not go to the woods with John?

Day 62

Lowercase W

In the block on your page, write a big letter W. Next to it write a whole row of little w. Little w stays between the lines. Circle your best one.

Subtracting with Objects

What is twelve minus five? Draw twelve circles and cross off five of them. How many are left?

$$12 - 5 = ?$$

SP

gasp   lisp   wisp

gasp risk   bent desk   milk task

wish   float   tie   know   rope   boat   try   won't   oar

shore   give   pole   don't   push   drag   funny

"Kate, I wish we had a boat to put the dolls in. Don't you?"

"I know what we can do. We can get the little tub, and tie a rope to it, and drag it to the pond. This will float with the dolls in it, and we can get a pole to push it from the shore."

Day 63

Lowercase Y

In the block on your page, write a big letter Y. Next to it write a whole row of little y. Little y has a tail that hangs down below the line. Circle your best one.

Adding with Objects

What is four plus three? Draw a picture that shows the equation. Then count them all up. How many are there all together?

$$4 + 3 = ?$$

belt held   felt mist   jump raft
bend gift   best melt   lift hand

I ran fast to hand the disk to the man.

Finish the story. *Marks where you left off.

"Kate, I wish we had a boat to put the dolls in. Don't you?"

"I know what we can do. We can get the little tub, and tie a rope to it, and drag it to the pond. This will float with the dolls in it, and we can get a pole to push it from the shore."*

"What a funny boat, Kate! A tub for a boat, and a pole for an oar! Won't it upset?"

"We can try it, Emma, and see."

"Well you get the tub, and I will get a pole and a rope. We will put both dolls in the tub, and give them a ride."

Day 64

Writing Words

Write the words: wavy, valley, win. Put your finger down to make a space between each word.

_____

_____

_____

_____

Subtracting with Objects

What is nine minus three? Draw a picture that shows the equation. How many are left?

$9 - 3 = ?$

Read across each row.

bent   tent   sent   dent   rent

fast   past   last   mast   vast

rest   pest   test   nest   best

bust   dust   rust   must   just

gift   lift   rift   sift

damp   lamp   camp   ramp

Day 65

Lowercase X

In the block on your page, write a big letter X. Next to it write a whole row of little x. Little x stays between the lines. Circle your best one.

Counting

Count the number of sets of footprints by ones. Then count the number of toes by tens. Then count the number of toes by fives.

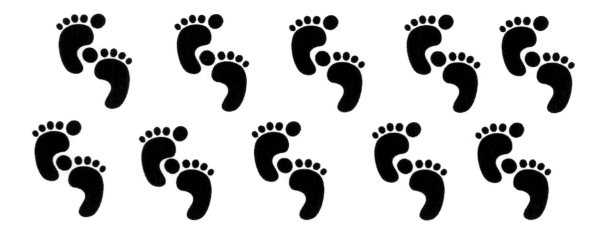

Read down each column.

bent	tent	sent	dent	rent
fast	past	last	mast	vast
rest	pest	test	nest	best
bust	dust	rust	must	just
gift	lift	rift	sift	
damp	lamp	camp	ramp	

Day 66

Lowercase Z

In the block on your page, write a big letter Z. Next to it write a whole row of little z. Little z stays between the lines. Circle your best one.

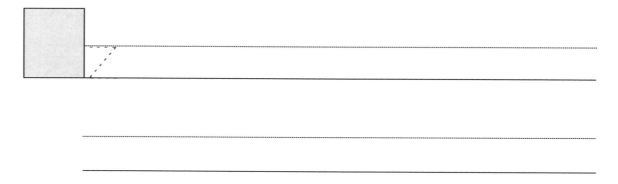

Adding with Objects

What is five plus two? Draw a picture that shows the equation. Then count them all up. How many are there all together?

5 + 2 = ?

Y

These words add -y without changing.

sand	sandy
milk	milky
pest	pesty
jump	jumpy

bound Rose called got drown found brave came
water Sandy jumped mouth around brought

"Here, Sandy! Here, Sandy!" Kate called to her dog. "Come, and get the dolls out of the pond."

Rose went under, but she did not drown. Olive was still on the top of the water.

Day 67

Writing Words

Write the words: zoo, box, zebra. Put your finger down to make a space between each word.

_____

_____

Subtracting with Objects

What is ten minus seven Draw a picture that shows the equation. How many are left?

10 - 7 = ?

These words change their spelling. How?

fun	funny
sun	sunny
run	runny
mud	muddy
pup	puppy
dad	daddy

Finish the story. *Shows where you left off.

"Here, Sandy! Here, Sandy!" Kate called to her dog. "Come, and get the dolls out of the pond."

Rose went under, but she did not drown. Olive was still on the top of the water.*

Sandy came with a bound, and jumped into the pond. He swam around, and got Olive in his mouth, and brought her to the shore.

Sandy then found Rose, and brought her out, too.

Kate said, "Good, old Sandy! Brave old dog!"

What do you think of Sandy?

Day 68

Writing

Write your first name. The first letter should be a big letter. The other letters should be little, lowercase letters.

Adding with Objects

What is four plus four? Draw a picture that shows the equation. Then count them all up. How many are there all together?

$4 + 4 = ?$

Y

silly Bobby
funny Penny
sandy Sammy
fuzzy Andy
muddy buddy
rusty daddy

June   Lucy   air   kind   trees   singing
blue   when   pure   says   sky   picnic

What a bright June day! The air is pure. The sky is as blue as it can be.

Lucy and her mama are in the woods. They have found a nice spot, where there is some grass.

Day 69

Practice

Trace the letter. Then fill the row with your own. Then write the matching uppercase letter in the block.

Subtracting with Objects

What is five minus three? Draw a picture that shows the equation. How many are left?

5 - 3 = ?

Y

jumpy nanny
lumpy kitty
sunny mommy
windy doggy
dusty puppy

The silly puppy can jump and run.

Finish the story. *Shows where you left off.

   What a bright June day! The air is pure. The sky is as blue as it can be.

   Lucy and her mama are in the woods. They have found a nice spot, where there is some grass.

   *They sit in the shade of the trees, and Lucy is singing.

   The trees are not large, but they make a good shade.

   Lucy's kind mama says that they will have a picnic when her papa can get a tent.

Day 70

Practice

Trace the letter. Then fill the row with your own. Then write the matching uppercase letter in the block.

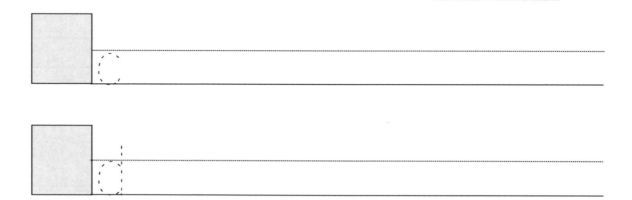

Count to 100.

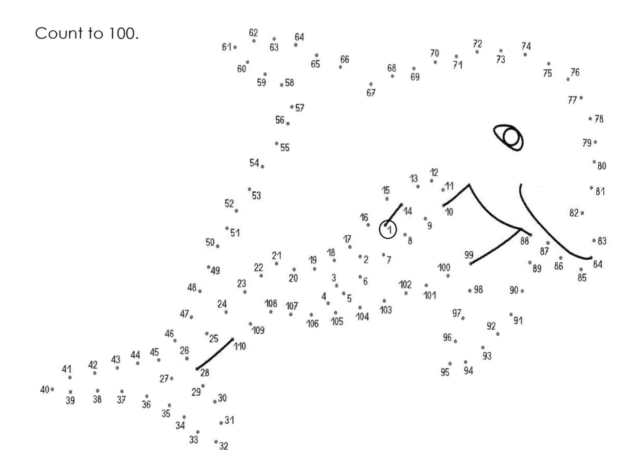

Doubles

Did you notice that on words with three letter we double the end letter to add a Y? Here are some other words with double letters.

bell   fell   hell   sell   tell

bill   dill   gill   hill   pill   will

dull   hull   mull

buzz   fuzz   fizz   jazz

buff   cuff   huff   muff   puff

bass   mass   pass   mess   miss   kiss

messy mess   fuzzy fuzz   fizzy fizz

The one below is a little different. The "a" has a different sound. Do you remember how to read the first word, *all*?

all   ball   call   fall   hall   tall

Practice

Trace the letter. Then fill the row with your own. Then write the matching uppercase letter in the block.

Adding and Subtracting with Ones and Zeros

If you have three cookies and I give you no more, how many do you have? You still have three. If you gave me zero cookies, how many would you have? You'd still have three. If I gave you one more cookie, how many would you have? Four. Then you gave me one of your cookies, how many would you have? Three.

5 − 0 =   6 − 1 =   4 + 1 =

4 + 0 =   2 + 1 =   5 − 1 =

3 + 1 =   7 + 0 =   9 − 0 =

SH

Here are two letters you see together a lot. Do you know what sound they make together? Put your finger to your mouth and let someone know they should be quiet. Sh!

bash	cash
dash	gash
hash	lash
mash	rash
sash	dish
fish	wish
hush	lush
mush	rush

fishy dish	fast cash	funny wish
rush golf	mad dash	Sh! Hush!

The messy fish is wet.

Practice

Trace the letter. Then fill the row with your own. Then write the matching uppercase letter in the block.

Adding and Subtracting with Two

If you have two cookies and I give you two more, how many do you have? Four. If you had four cookies, and you gave me two of them, how many would you have left? Two.

$4 - 2 =$ $3 - 1 =$ $5 + 1 =$

$2 + 2 =$ $2 + 1 =$ $4 - 2 =$

$2 + 1 =$ $7 - 0 =$ $8 - 1 =$

TH

Here are another two letters you see together a lot. To make this sound you have to stick out your tongue! The word that begins with a capital letter is a name. Names always begin with a capital letter.

bath

math

path

Beth

with

Seth

kitty bath   funny math   with cash

Math is fun with GC!

Dash fast on the muddy, buggy path!

Practice

Trace the letter. Then fill the row with your own. Then write the matching uppercase letter in the block.

Adding and Subtracting with Two

If you have four cookies and I give you two more, how many do you have? Start with four and count on two more. You would have six. Put up two fingers on one hand two four on the other. Does it matter if you add four plus two or two plus four? No, that's six either way. If you had six cookies and you gave me two of them, how many would you have left? Four. This time you just had to count back by two.

$4 - 2 =$ $6 - 2 =$ $2 + 4 =$

$2 + 2 =$ $2 + 4 =$ $4 + 2 =$

$4 + 2 =$ $4 - 2 =$ $6 - 2 =$

CH, TCH

These two letter combos above make the same sound.

bun   bunch
pun   punch
ben   bench
pin   pinch

lunch   such   rich   much

ba batch   pi pitch

match   patch
ditch   fetch

Fetch his lunch.

Pitch the ball or sit on the bench.

Catch them in the ditch.

Practice

Trace the letter. Then fill the row with your own. Then write the matching uppercase letter in the block.

Adding and Subtracting with Two

If you have two cookies and I give you three more, how many do you have? Five. If you had three cookies and I gave you two more, how many would you have? Five. Two plus three and three plus two have the same sum, five. Just start with the bigger number and count on the smaller number. If you had five cookies, and you gave me two of them, how many would you have left? Three.

$5 - 2 =$ $3 + 2 =$ $5 - 2 =$

$2 + 3 =$ $2 + 4 =$ $4 - 2 =$

$2 + 2 =$ $6 - 2 =$ $4 + 2 =$

Blends

bunch	bash	back	bill
ditch	dish	dock	doll
lunch	lush	luck	lull
hunch	hush	hack	hill
	wish	wick	will

pinch	path	pack	pill
match	mash	muck	math
with	bath	risk	duck
rash	lick	mist	posh

candy is yummy   happy math

windy path   sandy ditch

The sun set in the west.

This dish is rich.

Milk with lunch is best.

Practice

Trace the letter. Then fill the row with your own. Then write the matching uppercase letter in the block.

Adding with Two

Use the number line to add by two. Start at zero and add by two. You will be skip counting with the even numbers. Then start at one and add two over and over, skip counting along the odd numbers.

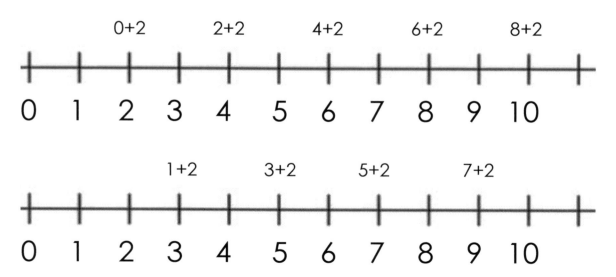

James and Robert have gone into the shade of a high wall to play ball.

Mary and Lucy have come up from the pond nearby, with brave old Sandy, to play too.

When they toss the ball up in the air, and try to catch it, Sandy runs to get it in his mouth.

Practice

Trace the letter. Then fill the row with your own. Then write the matching uppercase letter in the block.

o p

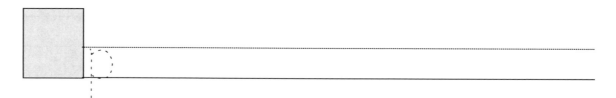

Adding with Two

5 + 2 =	3 + 2 =	2 + 5 =
2 + 1 =	2 + 4 =	7 + 2 =
2 + 2 =	2 + 6 =	2 + 3 =
6 + 2 =	8 + 2 =	0 + 2 =

ING

d	ing	ding
k	ing	king
r	ing	ring
s	ing	sing
th	ing	thing

The king can sing.

ANG

b	ang	bang
g	ang	gang
h	ang	hang
r	ang	rang
s	ang	sang

The gang sang.

Practice

Trace the letter. Then fill the row with your own. Then write the matching uppercase letter in the block.

Subtracting with Two

Use the number line to subtract by two. Start at ten and subtract by two. You will be skip counting with the even numbers. Then start at nine and subtract two over and over, skip counting along the odd numbers.

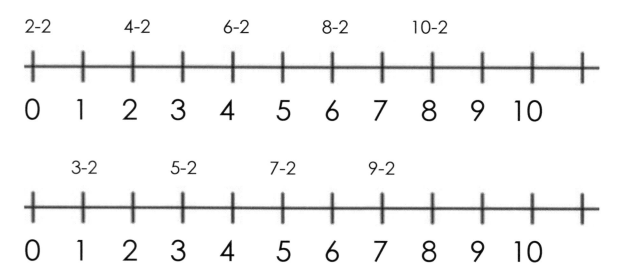

UNG

h	ung	hung
r	ung	rung
s	ung	sung

ONG

b	ong	bong
d	ong	dong
l	ong	long
s	ong	song

Sing a long song. I sang a long song.

Hang on a rung. I hung on a rung.

ding dong   ping pong   King Kong

Practice

Trace the letter. Then fill the row with your own. Then write the matching uppercase letter in the block.

s t

Subtracting with Two

5 – 2 =   3 - 2 =   9 - 2 =

8 - 2 =   4 - 2 =   7 – 2 =

2 - 2 =   6 - 2 =   10 - 2 =

10 - 2 =   8 – 2 =   6 - 2 =

ING

bang	ing	banging
jump	ing	jumping
sing	ing	singing
long	ing	longing

ringing	fetching
risking	pitching
helping	sending
fishing	packing
itching	hanging

I am jumping and singing.

Ben is pitching. Jen is catching. (Catch has a different
A sound, but you've seen that word before. Can you read catching?)

Penny is helping and packing.

Fishing in the pond is fun.

Practice

Trace the letter. Then fill the row with your own. Then write the matching uppercase letter in the block.

Add and Subtracting with Two

5 – 2 =   2 + 3 =   9 - 2 =

8 + 2 =   4 - 2 =   2 + 7 =

2 - 2 =   6 - 2 =   10 - 2 =

10 - 2 =   8 – 2 =   6 + 2 =

INK

l	ink	link
p	ink	pink
r	ink	rink
s	ink	sink
w	ink	wink
th	ink	think
w	ink	wink ing winking

ANK

b	ank	bank	s	ank	sank
t	ank	tank	th	ank	thank

I am thinking.

I am thanking Jen.

The bank is pink. The rink is red.

Practice

Trace the letter. Then fill the row with your own. Then write the matching uppercase letter in the block.

Adding and Subtracting

Use the number line to add and subtract. Start at one and add three and then subtract three. You'll end up back at one. Then start at two and add four and then subtract four. Count up and back. You'll end up back at two. Adding and subtracting are opposites.

$3 + 5 = 8$ and $5 + 3 = 8$ and $8 - 3 = 5$ and $8 - 5 = 3$

We call that a fact family. 3, 5, 8 are an addition and subtraction fact family. 2, 4, 6 are also a fact family. Add and subtract to show it. Count up and down to show $2 + 4 = 6$ and $4 + 2 = 6$ and $6 - 2 = 4$ and $6 - 4 = 2$. Find more fact families.

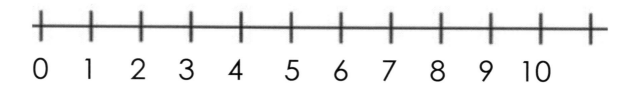

James and Robert have gone into the shade of a high wall to play ball.

Mary and Lucy have come up from the pond nearby, with brave old Sandy, to see them play.

When they toss the ball up in the air, and try to catch it, Sandy runs to get it in his mouth.

Now the ball is lost. They all look for it under the trees and in the grass; but they cannot see it. Where can it be?

See! Sandy has found it. Here he comes with it. He will lay it at little Lucy's feet, or put it in her hand.

Practice

Trace the letter. Then fill the row with your own. Then write the matching uppercase letter in the block.

Three Plus Three Equals Six

3 + 3 =	3 + 2 =	1 + 3 =
2 + 3 =	4 + 2 =	7 + 2 =
2 + 2 =	3 + 3 =	8 + 2 =
3 + 3 =	0 + 2 =	2 + 3 =

UNK

b	unk	bunk	d	unk	dunk
f	unk	funk	g	unk	gunk
h	unk	hunk	p	unk	punk
s	unk	sunk	j	unk	junk

ing	sing	singing
ink	sink	sinking
ank	bank	banking
unk	dunk	dunking
ink	wink	winking
ank	thank	thanking
unk	junk	junking

I am jumping on the bunk bed.

I can dunk the ball.

Name and Address

Write your name and address as best as you can.

_____

_____

_____

_____

_____

_____

Six Minus Three Equals Three
(This is the opposite of 3 + 3 = 6.)

6 - 3 =   3 - 2 =   6 - 3 =

8 - 2 =   4 - 2 =   6 - 2 =

5 - 2 =   6 - 3 =   10 - 2 =

3 - 3 =   7 - 2 =   6 - 1 =

When A Says Its Name

can   cane   hat   hate
tap   tape   Jan   Jane
pan   pane   mad   made

sale   wave   safe
game   gate   name

Notice the spelling on these next ones:

back bake   lack lake
sack sake   rack rake

made a date   bake a cake

fake name   safe at lake

bake sale   rate the game

thanking Jane   helping rake

Zero

Write the word zero. Then trace the zero and write a full row of them.

0

Three Plus Four Equals Seven (And four plus three equals seven. Say it both ways.)

3 + 4 =   7 + 2 =   4 + 3 =

2 + 4 =   3 + 3 =   6 + 2 =

2 + 2 =   2 + 5 =   8 + 2 =

3 + 4 =   5 + 2 =   2 + 7 =

When I Says Its Name

bit   bite   dim   dime
fin   fine   hid   hide
kit   kite   rid   ride
win   wine   rip   ripe

Notice the spelling on these:

fill   file   pill   pile

mill   mile   lick   like

life in a mine   ride a kite

Hide nine dimes in a pile.

I like ripe limes.

I like the fine kite I made.

Ride a mile on the lake.

One

Write the word one. Then trace the one and write a full row of them.

Seven Minus Three Equals Four (And seven minus four equals three. Say it both ways.)

4 - 3 =   7 - 4 =   7 - 3 =

8 - 2 =   4 - 2 =   7 - 2 =

2 - 1 =   6 - 3 =   5 - 2 =

7 - 4 =   6 - 3 =   7 - 3 =

When O Says Its Name

hop   hope   rob   robe

rod   rode   not   note

home   code   poke   nope   woke

hope   lone   cone   rope   pole

Notice the spelling change on this: jock   joke

mole home   note in code

I hope it is a joke.

The mole made a home in the hole.

I woke and rode home.

The pole is in the hole at Mile Lake.

The yummy cone fell at lunch.

Two

Write the word two. Then trace the two and write a full row of them.

2

Three Plus Five Equals Eight

3 + 4 =   3 + 5 =   4 + 3 =

2 + 4 =   3 + 3 =   6 + 2 =

2 + 2 =   3 + 5 =   3 + 3 =

5 + 3 =   3 + 4 =   2 + 7 =

When O Says Its Name

Here's a time when O says its name when it is written all by itself.
Read these examples:

old	bold	fold	gold
hold	mold	sold	told
bolt	colt	host	most

The lime is old and moldy.

Take this roll and hold on to it.

The most fun is running and jumping.

Fold it and put it here.

He mines for gold here.

The colt sold fast.

Three

Write the word three. Then trace the three and write a full row of them.

3

Eight Minus Three Equals Five

4 - 3 =   8 - 3 =   7 - 3 =

8 - 5 =   4 - 2 =   7 - 2 =

6 - 3 =   5 - 2 =   7 - 4 =

8 - 3 =   6 - 0 =   8 - 5 =

When U Says Its Name

Say the word pairs. Can you hear the difference between them?

cub cube   cut cute   us use

The second word in each pair says, "Yoo."

Now read these word pairs. Can you hear the difference between them and the first words?

tub tube   duck duke

The second word in each pair says, "Oo."

rude joke   use tube   cute duke

The duke will rule.

Luke is rude.

Use the tube to cure it.

He fumes if he is mad.

The cute puppy is licking the bone.

Four

Write the word four. Then trace the four and write a full row of them.

4

Four Plus Four Equals Eight

4 + 4 =   3 + 5 =   4 + 3 =

2 + 4 =   3 + 3 =   2 + 0 =

3 + 4 =   1 + 3 =   5 + 3 =

4 + 4 =   3 + 4 =   2 + 7 =

When E Says Its Name

We've been adding an "e" to the end of words to make a vowel say its name.

Here are some words for E: *here* and *Eve*.

If you have played on Starfall.com, then maybe you know the song, "When two vowels go a walking, the first one does the talking." In other words, when two vowels are together, the first vowel says its name.

Here are some examples with E.

bee	beef	beep	beet
Dee	deep	deer	
fee	feed	feel	feet
pee	peep	peer	
see	seed	seen	
wee	weed	week	weep

Five

Write the word five. Then trace the five and write a full row of them.

5

Eight Minus Four Equals Four

4 - 1 =   8 - 4 =   7 - 3 =

8 - 5 =   4 - 2 =   7 - 4 =

5 - 2 =   8 - 3 =   6 - 2 =

8 - 4 =   6 - 0 =   8 - 5 =

When E Says Its Name

Here are words that are spelled, EA. They are two vowels together, so the first one is going to say its name. E comes first so when you see EA, you read the E sound.

bead	beam	beat
deal	dear	
heal	heap	heat
lead	leap	lean
meal	mean	meat
team	tear	
weak	wean	

I like eating meat.

The red team is in the lead.

The sentences below use different words that sound the same. Which two words sound the same? Which word is which?

Each week in the heat I feel weak.

Dear mom, I see a deer.

I eat a beet. I hear a beat.

Six

Write the word six. Then trace the six and write a full row of them.

6

Four Plus Five Equals Nine

4 + 4 =   4 + 5 =   5 + 4 =

2 + 4 =   3 + 5 =   2 + 2 =

5 + 4 =   5 + 3 =   4 + 5 =

2 + 5 =   4 + 3 =   2 + 7 =

When E Says Its Name

Here's another time E says its name, when it's all by itself at the end of a two-letter word. Read these examples:

be   he   me   we   she

The last one is different! It has three letters, but the *s* and *h* only make one sound.

O can do this as well—no, go, so, but not to or do!

She is eating a red beet.

I can hear mine beating.

He will reach home so fast.

He is teaching pitching.

We ride miles on neat bikes.

No, bake a cube cake and feed me it.

Go dig a hole and fill it back in with mud.

Do not be here late!

Seven

Write the word seven. Then trace the seven and write a full row of them.

7

Nine Minus Four Equals Five

9 - 4 =   8 - 4 =   7 - 4 =

8 - 5 =   4 - 2 =   7 - 3 =

7 - 1 =   5 - 3 =   9 - 5 =

9 - 4 =   9 - 5 =   8 - 3 =

care   always   line   Frank   row   been   keeps   home

Frank has a pretty boat. It is white, with a black line near the water.

He keeps it in the pond, near his home. He always takes good care of it.

Frank has been at work in the garden, and will now row awhile.

Eight

Write the word eight. Then trace the eight and write a full row of them.

8

Five Plus Five Equals Ten

4 + 4 =   4 + 5 =   5 + 4 =

5 + 5 =   3 + 5 =   2 + 2 =

2 + 0 =   5 + 4 =   5 + 3 =

4 + 5 =   5 + 5 =   4 + 2 =

4 + 3 =   2 + 1 =   2 + 8 =

When I Says Its Name

Read these examples where I says its name:

find   **hind**   **kind**
mind   **mild**   **wild**

Here are two similar examples with I and O:

tiny   **pony**

The kind, old man is Dan.

The wild, tiny boy is Dave.

His pony is mild and his fish is sick.

His mind is quick and his feet, fast.

Can she find me here in this shop?

Be kind to him.

The moldy roll will make me sick.

We told him kindly to be here at sun up.

Nine

Write the word nine. Then trace the nine and write a full row of them.

9

Ten Minus Five Equals Five

9 - 4 =   8 - 4 =   7 - 4 =

10 - 5 =   8 - 5 =   7 - 3 =

7 - 1 =   5 - 3 =   9 - 5 =

6 - 2 =   3 - 2 =   8 - 4 =

6 - 0 =   10 - 5 =   8 - 3 =

Long and Short

Read these examples with words with both the long and short vowel sounds. When the vowel says its name, we call that the long vowel sound.

Will he tell a tall tale?

Hug a cute puppy.

Pop in at home and eat lunch.

His dad has a job at home.

His big kick will win the game.

Sit with me here and sip hot tea.

His cat will gulp a bug in the sun.

It is time to go, so ride home.

The lone kid sat and ate.

At the game, catch the ball in the mitt.

Ten

Write the word ten. Trace the ten. Then put your finger down next to it. On the other side of your finger write the next ten. Leave a finger width's space between each ten. Write a full row of them.

10

Adding 0, 1, 2, 3, 4, 5

5 + 0 =	1 + 3 =	1 + 4 =
2 + 5 =	2 + 3 =	2 + 2 =
3 + 5 =	3 + 4 =	3 + 3 =
2 + 4 =	4 + 3 =	4 + 4 =
3 + 5 =	5 + 5 =	5 + 4 =

ING

When we added E onto the end of short words like *bit*, making it *bite*, the E made the I say its name.

To make the word bite – ing, we write *biting*. The second vowel makes the first say its name.

But sometimes we don't want the vowel to say its name!

To write hug – ing, we write *hugging*. We put in a double letter to keep the vowels apart so the second vowel doesn't make the first vowel says its name.

Read these examples of double letter words:

bed	bedding
bet	betting
fan	fanning
fit	fitting
get	getting
hop	hopping
hum	humming

Eleven

Write the word eleven. Trace eleven and write a full row. Leave a finger width's space between each eleven.

Subtracting 0, 1, 2, 3, 4, 5

$5 - 1 =$ $1 - 0 =$ $4 - 1 =$

$6 - 2 =$ $5 - 2 =$ $7 - 2 =$

$8 - 3 =$ $6 - 3 =$ $4 - 3 =$

$7 - 4 =$ $8 - 4 =$ $9 - 4 =$

$5 - 5 =$ $8 - 5 =$ $7 - 5 =$

Double Letters

jig	jigging
let	letting
map	mapping
mop	mopping
pop	popping

The words below don't need an extra letter. Why?

limp	limping
jump	jumping
bump	bumping
help	helping
tell	telling

I like telling time.

I like helping with mopping.

The hopping and jumping game is fun.

I must get the puppy bedding.

Twelve

Write the word twelve. Then trace the twelve and write a full row of them. Don't forget to leave a space between each one you write.

12

Adding 0, 1, 2, 3, 4, 5

5 + 1 =   0 + 3 =   1 + 6 =

5 + 2 =   2 + 4 =   2 + 6 =

3 + 4 =   2 + 3 =   3 + 3 =

4 + 4 =   4 + 2 =   5 + 4 =

2 + 5 =   4 + 5 =   5 + 5 =

LESSON XXXVII.

much   one   yet   hungry   seen   grandma   corn   would

"What is that?" said Lucy, as she came out on the steps. "Oh, it is a little boat! What a pretty one it is!"

"I will give it to you when it is finished," said John, kindly. "Would you like to have it?"

"Yes, very much, thank you, John. Has grandma seen it?"

"Not yet; we will take it to her by and by. What do you have in your pan, Lucy?"

"Some corn for my hens, John. They must be very hungry."

Thirteen

Write the word thirteen. Then trace the thirteen and write a full row of them.
Don't forget to leave a space between each one.

13

Subtracting 0, 1, 2, 3, 4, 5

3 - 1 =	1 - 1 =	8 - 1 =
7 - 2 =	6 - 2 =	5 - 2 =
7 - 3 =	5 - 3 =	3 - 3 =
9 - 4 =	5 - 4 =	6 - 4 =
10 - 5 =	9 – 5 =	7 – 5 =

ED

Now we are going to take some of these same words and add an ED to the end of them.

These words you say with a "D" sound on the end.

fan	fanning	fanned
hum	humming	hummed
bag	bagging	bagged
tan	tanning	tanned

These words you say with a "T" sound on the end.

mop	mopping	mopped
pop	popping	popped
limp	limping	limped
jump	jumping	jumped
bump	bumping	bumped
help	helping	helped
hop	hopping	hopped
map	mapping	mapped

Fourteen

Write the word fourteen. Then trace the fourteen and write a full row of them.

Adding 0, 1, 2, 3, 4, 5

$0 + 0 =$ $1 + 1 =$ $6 + 1 =$

$2 + 2 =$ $4 + 2 =$ $5 + 2 =$

$3 + 2 =$ $3 + 5 =$ $3 + 3 =$

$3 + 4 =$ $4 + 4 =$ $4 + 2 =$

$4 + 5 =$ $5 + 3 =$ $5 + 5 =$

ED

Say these words with an "ED" sound at the end.

fit	fitting	fitted
melt	melting	melted
end	ending	ended

He helped with fitting the hat.

He fanned me to make me cold.

I bumped into the desk and the milk fell.

She melted the butter to make the cake.

Fifteen

Write the word fifteen. Then trace the fifteen and write a full row of them.

15

Subtracting 0, 1, 2, 3, 4, 5

10 - 1 =	4 - 0 =	6 - 1 =
4 - 2 =	3 - 2 =	6 - 2 =
7 - 3 =	5 - 3 =	3 - 3 =
6 - 4 =	5 - 4 =	8 - 4 =
5 - 5 =	7 – 5 =	8 – 5 =

ER

Now we are going to take some of these same words and add an ER to the end of them.

fan	fanning	fanned	fanner
bag	bagging	bagged	bagger
hum	humming	hummed	hummer
tan	tanning	tanned	tanner
hop	hopping	hopped	hopper
limp	limping	limped	limper
jump	jumping	jumped	jumper
help	helping	helped	helper
kick	kicking	kicked	kicker

Did you notice all the double letters? They don't all have double letters, which ones do? They *do* all have two letters between the first and second vowel.

Sixteen

Write the word sixteen. Then trace the sixteen and write a full row of them.

16

Adding 0, 1, 2, 3, 4, 5

2 + 1 =	0 + 3 =	1 + 5 =
2 + 3 =	2 + 2 =	2 + 4 =
3 + 4 =	3 + 3 =	2 + 3 =
4 + 4 =	4 + 2 =	4 + 5 =
5 + 5 =	2 + 5 =	5 + 3 =

Review

The bagger bagged the meat and milk.

The tanner tanned the hide of a deer.

I am a helper at home with mom and dad.

The kicker is kicking the ball.

He hummed and ate all the cake.

The fastest hopper is the winner.

Lending a hand helps a lot.

Winter is wetter than summer.

Seventeen

Write the word seventeen. Then trace the number and write a full row of them.

7

Subtracting 0, 1, 2, 3, 4, 5

$3 - 0 =$ $3 - 1 =$ $8 - 1 =$

$6 - 2 =$ $7 - 2 =$ $4 - 2 =$

$8 - 3 =$ $5 - 3 =$ $7 - 3 =$

$7 - 4 =$ $9 - 4 =$ $6 - 4 =$

$6 - 5 =$ $9 - 5 =$ $8 - 5 =$

market   bread   basket   bought

meat   tea   trying   tell   which

A special note: The EA in bread does not say E. It makes the short E sound like the words head and heaven.

James has been to market with his mama.

She has bought some bread, some meat, and some tea, which are in the basket on her arm.

James is trying to tell his mama what he has seen in the market.

Eighteen

Write the word eighteen. Then trace the eighteen and write a full row of them.

18

Adding and Subtracting

$3 + 0 =$ $1 + 5 =$ $7 - 3 =$

$2 + 3 =$ $2 + 2 =$ $4 - 2 =$

$3 + 4 =$ $3 + 2 =$ $3 - 3 =$

$5 + 4 =$ $4 + 3 =$ $8 - 4 =$

$2 + 5 =$ $5 + 3 =$ $9 - 5 =$

ING and ER and ED

Sometimes we want the first vowel to say its name, like with *biting*. We want the I to say its name. If we added a double T, what would it say?

bit-ting – That's not a word!

Read these examples with NO double letters, so all of the first vowels say their name.

bite ing	biting	biter
ride ing	riding	rider
mine ing	mining	miner

mope	moping	moper	moped
vote	voting	voter	voted
rope	roping	roper	roped
hate	hating	hater	hated
rate	rating	rater	rated
rake	raking	raker	raked

Nineteen

Write the word nineteen. Then trace the nineteen and write a full row of them.

19

Adding and Subtracting

5 - 0 =	4 + 1 =	2 + 4 =
5 - 2 =	1 + 2 =	5 + 2 =
6 - 3 =	3 + 2 =	5 + 3 =
7 - 4 =	4 + 5 =	3 + 4 =
10 - 5 =	3 + 5 =	5 + 5 =

ING and ER

read	reading	reader	
lead	leading	leader	
bead	beading	beaded	
leap	leaping	leaper	leaped

Reading is fun.

I voted. I like the leader.

Riding fast, we feel the wind go past.

The miner is at his home near the mine.

Twenty

Write the word twenty. Then trace the twenty and write a full row of them.

20

Adding and Subtracting

9 - 5 =   1 + 1 =   1 + 4 =

6 - 2 =   2 + 5 =   6 + 2 =

3 - 1 =   3 + 4 =   5 + 3 =

6 - 4 =   4 + 2 =   4 + 3 =

8 - 5 =   5 + 5 =   5 + 4 =

Long and Short

hop	hopping	hopped
hope	hoping	hoped
mop	mopping	mopped
mope	moping	moped
tap	tapping	tapped
tape	taping	taped
back	backing	backed
bake	baking	baked
fill	filling	filled
file	filing	filed

Writing Words

Write these words: lunch, pitch, match, rich, such.

_____

_____

_____

_____

Adding and Subtracting

0 + 6 =	7 - 6 =	10 + 0 =
2 + 4 =	7 - 7 =	8 + 2 =
3 + 4 =	8 - 3 =	3 + 3 =
5 + 4 =	7 - 2 =	4 + 3 =
4 + 5 =	8 - 4 =	5 + 2 =

Sentences

I am a renter and I rented a home here.

I taped the sheet up to make a tent.

The cake filling is yummy.

I am hoping that I am hopping the fastest.

He backed up and fell in the ditch!

He moped all the time.

The rider must help us.

He is lending me a hand by helping to mop.

Summer is sunny and winter is chilly.

Writing Words

Write these words: bath, pack, will, munch, dash.

_____

_____

_____

_____

_____

Adding and Subtracting

8 + 0 =	2 + 1 =	9 - 8 =
2 + 3 =	2 + 5 =	4 - 2 =
3 + 5 =	3 + 3 =	10 - 5 =
4 + 3 =	4 + 4 =	9 - 4 =
1 + 5 =	5 + 3 =	7 - 2 =

reads   so   wears   please   could   hair   fast
love   easy   gray   chair   who   glasses

See my dear, old grandma in her easy chair! How gray her hair is! She wears glasses when she reads.

She is always kind, and takes such good care of me that I like to do what she tells me.

When she says, "Robert, will you get me a drink?" I run as fast as I can to get it for her. Then she says, "Thank you, my boy."

Would you not love a dear, good grandma, who is so kind? And would you not do all you could to please her?

Writing Words

Write these words: ring, thing, king, sang, bang.

_____

_____

_____

_____

Word Problems

If you had two goldfish in your tank and bought three more fish from the store, how many fish would you have all together? You could draw a picture to help you find the answer.

If you had a box of five crayons and took out two of them, how many would be left in the box? You could draw a picture to help you find the answer.

Chunk that Word!

You can break up big words and read their parts.

itself	it-self
cannot	can-not
bedtime	bed-time
sunset	sun-set
forget	for-get
salamander	sal-a-man-der
cupcake	cup-cake
baseball	base-ball
rabbit	rab-bit
pumpkin	pump-kin
talented	tal-en-ted

Writing Words

Write these words: rung, song, hung, long, sang.

Word Problems

If you had three dogs and brought home two cats, how many pets would you have all together? You could draw a picture to help you find the answer.

If you had six carrots on your plate and ate two of them, how many would be left on your plate? You could draw a picture to help you find the answer.

More than One

Add an S

ball	balls	wall	walls
bike	bikes	rake	rakes
cat	cats	hat	hats
dog	dogs	mug	mugs
hit	hits	pit	pits
kid	kids	bid	bids
lock	locks	rock	rocks

Add an ES

patch	patches	pitch	pitches
wish	wishes	rash	rashes
buzz	buzzes	fizz	fizzes
lunch	lunches	bunch	bunches

Writing Words

Write these words: catching, jumping, sending, hanging.

_____

_____

_____

_____

_____

_____

Word Problems

If you had four aunts and uncles and five cousins and they were all coming for dinner, how many people would be coming over? Can you write the math equation like 1 + 2 = 3?

If you had eight cookies and shared five of them, how many would you have left? Can you write the math equation, something like 4 - 2 = 2?

X

box (rhymes with socks)

fox

fix

fax

tax (sounds like tacks)

tux

exit   ex-it

expect   ex-pect

exterminate   ex-ter-min-ate

I expect him to fix his box.

I came in the exit!

Writing Words

Write these sentences: The bank is pink. The rink is red.

_____

_____

_____

_____

_____

_____

Word Problems

If you picked four strawberries and then picked four more, how many would you have all together? Can you write the math equation like 1 + 2 = 3?

If you had six songs to sing in your concert and had already sung three, how many songs did you have left to sing? Can you write the math equation, something like 4 - 2 = 2?

SH

shut	ship	shape	shop
share	shot	shell	shade
shake	shave	she	shed
sheet	shelf	Sherry	shellfish

shock	shocked	shocking	shocker
shift	shifted	shifting	
shine	shined	shining	

I expect to find that the shearer shaved the sheep.

The sun is shining, so I am sitting in the shade.

Writing Words

Write these words: sunk, hunk, wink, thank, sinking.

Word Problems

Come up with a question that needs you to add or subtract to answer it. Draw a picture to show the question and write the math equation it shows.

does   wonder   mother   other

bee   honey   listen   flower

"Come here, Lucy, and listen! What is in this flower?"

"O mother! It is a bee. I wonder how it came to be shut up in the flower!"

"It went into the flower for some honey, and it may be it went to sleep. Then the flower shut it in."

"The bee likes honey as well as we do, but it does not like to be shut up in the flower."

"Should we let it out, Lucy?"

"Yes; then it can go to other flowers, and get honey."

Writing Words

Write these pairs of words. Put your finger down to make a space between the words.

mad made - tap tape - can cane - back bake

Coins

2 + 5 =   8 − 5 =   4 + 5 =

This is a penny.   It is worth one cent. We write 1₵.

Two pennies is worth two cents, 2₵.

How many pennies are below? How many cents are they worth?

                              _____

SH

wish shape   fish ship   shake shop

sell shell   rush shot   she gushed

Sherry shined   shudder shock

yummy dish   sunny shape

I rushed to the shop; I needed dishes.

The sun shone on the sand and shells.

I am shining my ship.

She's shaping up.

That is shocking!

I am eating a yummy dish at the Fish Shack.

Writing Words

Write these pairs of words. Put your finger down to make a space between the words.

bit bite - hid hide - fill file - lick like

_____

_____

_____

_____

Coins

2 + 5 =   7 − 5 =   4 + 3 =

This is a nickel. It is worth five cents. We write 5¢.

Two nickels is worth ten cents, 10¢.

How many nickels are below? How many cents are they worth? (Hint: count by fives.)

_____

CH

chips	chipper	chipping
chop	chopper	chopping
chatter	chatterer	chattering
chapped	cheep	cheap
cheat	cheer	chat
chase	check	checkers

Did she cheat at checkers?

I got chips cheap and cheered.

Check if he is chopping the cheese.

(The S in cheese sounds like a Z. You've seen that before with plural words such as fizzes and peaches.)

She is chattering to me.

Writing Words

Write these pairs of words. Put your finger down to make a space between the words.

hop hope - not note - lone home - jock joke

Coins

2 + 5 =   7 − 5 =   4 + 3 =

How much are these coins worth? Write the number of cents next to each line of coins.

_____

_____

CH

pitch chips   batch chopped

ditch checked   rich and cheap

Chase me!

The teacher checked the tests.

She chops trees for her job.

Run and fetch a bag of chips.

The dish is rich and yummy.

Find shade in the ditch.

Bake a batch of muffins.

Rent a cheap tent to pitch near the lake.

Writing Words

Write these pairs of words on each line. Put your finger down to make a space between the words.

cub cube - duck duke - us use - cut cute

_____

_____

_____

Coins

$3 + 4 =$ $6 - 2 =$ $2 + 3 =$

How much are these coins worth? Write the number of cents next to each line of coins. Count by fives and then count on by one.

WH

when   wheat   white   whiz

whip   whim   which   whopper

There are some wh and w words that don't follow the rules we've learned. You should just know them:

why who whose what

where weather were was

When did he leave his job?

Which were the games she liked best?

Whose bike was at home?

What team has a white logo? (lo-go)

Where was the whiz kid who likes math?

Who told that whopper of a tale?

Why is the weather so cold?

Writing Sentences

Copy the sentence. Make sure to leave space between the words.

In the heat I feel weak each week.

_____

_____

_____

_____

Coins

2 + 5 =   7 − 5 =   4 + 3 =

This is a dime. It is worth ten cents. We write 10₵.

Two dimes is worth twenty cents, 20₵.

How many dimes are below? How many cents are they worth? (Hint: count by tens.)

_____

best   hitched   their   or   riding

live   holds   hay   driving   tight   early

Here come Frank and James White. Do you know where they live?

Frank is riding a horse, and James is driving one hitched to a cart. They are out very early in the day. How happy they are!

See how well Frank rides, and how tight James holds the lines!

The boys should be kind to their horses. It is not best to whip them. When they have done riding, they will give the horses some hay or corn.

Writing Sentences

Copy the sentence. Make sure to leave space between the words.

He is teaching pitching.

....

_____

....

_____

....

_____

Coins

$3 + 5 =$ $\qquad$ $9 - 5 =$ $\qquad$ $3 + 3 =$

How much are these coins worth? Write the number of cents next to each line of coins. Count by tens and then count on by one and by five.

     _____

     _____

TH

then   this   that   those

these   thin   thick   thud

them   there (rhymes with where)

this, that and the other

These bells sing songs.

This bathtub was deep.

The weather is thick with fog.

Then hand this to them.

Those fans were cheering wildly.

There is the thin path that leads home.

The thick mud was under Beth's feet.

There is an S on the end of Beth's name. There is not more than one Beth. That mark is called an apostrophe. The apostrophe S tells us that the feet belong to Beth. They are Beth's feet.

Writing Sentences

Copy the sentence. Make sure to leave space between the words.

Take hold of his hand.

....

_____

....

_____

....

_____

Coins

$$4 + 5 = \qquad 8 - 5 = \qquad 3 + 4 =$$

How much are these coins worth? Write the number of cents next to each line of coins. Count by tens and then count on by one and by five.

    _____

     _____

QU

quick   quit   queen   quite
quilt   quack   quiet (qu – I – et)

I think I hear a duck quacking.

It was quite quiet here.

Quick, let's bake a cake.

I like soft quilts.

I quit thinking bad things.

They were quite wonderful.

Thank Sally for the queen-sized quilt.

Writing Sentences

Copy the sentence. Make sure to leave space between the words.

Can he find me here in this shop?

....

_____

....

_____

....

_____

Coins

$2 + 3 =$ $\qquad$ $7 - 3 =$ $\qquad$ $4 + 4 =$

This is a quarter.  It is worth twenty-five cents. We write 25¢.

Two quarters are worth fifty cents, 50¢.

Three quarters are worth 75¢. Four quarters are worth 100¢.

 _____

Review

When is he going to see the queen?

When is the best time to quit?

What is he thinking?

Where was she chasing him so quickly?

The cabins were quiet to rest in.

Rabbits do not quack.

Sherry is chomping on her lunch.

I like this cheese so much!

Let's sit in the shade; the weather is sunny.

Which lake is the best?

Writing Sentences

Copy the sentence. Make sure to leave space between the words.

His big kite will win the game.

Coins

4 + 4 =   7 – 5 =   2 + 5 =

How much are these coins worth? Write the number of cents next to each line of coins. Always start with the largest amount and then count on from there.

     _____

L Blends

a	la	bla	blab	blabber
a	la	fla	flap	flapping
a	la	pla	plan	planned
a	la	cla	clap	clapping
a	la	gla	glad	gladden
a	la	sla	slap	slapped

bleed	bleep	blubber	blame
fleet	flame	flip	flop
flute	flume	pluck	plate
plane	clear	plug	plugging

He claps his hands if he is happy.

The duck was flapping its wings.

Writing Words

Write these words: getting, popping, fitting, helping, telling.

....

_____

....

_____

....

_____

....

_____

Coins

4 + 2 =   5 – 3 =   5 + 4 =

How much are these coins worth? Write the number of cents next to each line of coins. Count by tens and then count on fives and ones.

     _____

looking   thought   picking   heard

chirp   were   told   search   dearly

young   girl   loved   birds   children   besides

A little girl went in search of flowers for her mother. It was early in the day, and the grass was wet. Sweet little birds were singing all around her.

And what do you think she found besides flowers? A nest with young birds in it.

While she was looking at them, she heard the mother bird chirp, as if she said, "Do not touch my children, little girl, for I love them dearly."

The little girl now thought how dearly her own mother loved her. So she left the birds. Then picking some flowers, she went home and told her mother what she had seen and heard.

Writing Words

Write these words: hummed, jumped, melted, fanned, mapped.

....

_____

....

_____

....

_____

Time

$$2 + 2 = \qquad 7 - 3 = \qquad 2 + 4 =$$

What time is it? The short hand points to the hour. We call this four o'clock. The short hand is pointing to the four. The long hand is pointing to the twelve.

L Blends

clean	cleaner	cleaned	cleaning
clog	clogger	clogged	clogging
clear	clearer	cleared	clearing
slip	slipper	slipped	slipping
sled	sleds	sledded	sledding
clutch	clutches	clutched	clutching
gleam	glum	sleep	sleeping
slug	slit	slab	slush

I slid in the slush after sledding.

I cleaned it and cleared the glob from the clog.

The slug gleamed in the sunny clearing.

Writing Words

Write these words: tanner, kicker, bagger, jumper, helper.

_____

_____

_____

_____

Time

$2 + 5 =$ $9 - 4 =$ $3 + 5 =$

What time is it? What number is the short hand pointing to?

_____ o'clock

L Blends

clean flag	flip slab	glad plan
slip slide	glum glad	plug clog
blame plane	sleep fleet	clip clop
pluck blob	blip bleep	slip shod

gleaming shine

flipping fantastic

I am sleepy. Please be quiet so I can go to sleep. (The S in please sounds like a Z like in cheese.)

I like flip flops on the sandy beach.

I pluck the weeds near the plants.

I am glad when the sun is shining.

I cleaned there and I need to clean here.

Writing Words

Write these words: reader, rider, leading, raking, voted, leaped.

_____

_____

_____

_____

Time

4 + 5 =   9 − 5 =   3 + 2 =

What time is it? What number is the short hand pointing to?

_____ o'clock

a	ma	sma	smash
e	me	sme	smell
i	mi	smi	smitten
o	mo	smo	smock
u	mu	smu	Smuckers

smile   smear   smack   smashing

a	na	sna	snap
e	ne	sne	Snell
i	ni	sni	snip
o	no	sno	snob
u	nu	snu	snub

snipe   sneer   snapping

I am smitten with the smell of lunch.

I smile when I think of him.

She got a smear on her smock.

Writing Words

Write these words: back, backing, backed, bake, baking, baked.

_____

_____

_____

_____

_____

_____

Time

5 + 5 =   8 − 5 =   3 + 4 =

What time is it? What number is the short hand pointing to?

_____ o'clock

ST, SP

e	te	ste	step
i	ti	sti	still
o	to	sto	stop
u	tu	stu	stuck
a	pa	spa	spat
e	pe	spe	sped

stick	stale	speed	spare
spine	steer	spade	stiff

I stepped in mud and got stuck.

I steered the clean, speedy rocket.

He smiled and stopped near the spitting llama. (I put in a funny-looking word. Can you guess what it is?)

Writing Words

Write these words: itself, cannot, bedtime, sunset, forget.

_____

_____

_____

_____

Time

$$4 + 2 = \qquad 7 - 5 = \qquad 6 + 2 =$$

What time is it? What number is the short hand pointing to?

_____ o'clock

eight   ask   after   town   past   ah   ticket
right   half   two   train   ding   lightning

"Mama, will you go to town?"

"What do you ask for a ticket on your train?"

"Oh! we will give you a ticket, mama."

"About what time will you get back?"

"At half past eight."

"Ah! that is after bedtime. Is this the fast train?"

"Yes, this is the lightning train."

"Oh! that is too fast for me."

"What should we get for you in town, mama?"

"A big basket, with two good little children in it."

"All right! Time is up! Ding, ding!"

Writing Words

Write these words: bikes, dogs, rocks, wishes, lunches, pitches.

Geometry

5 + 2 =   7 − 5 =   3 + 3 =

This is a square.
It has four sides.

Draw your own square.

SC, SK

a   can   scan
i   kit   skit

Kate	skate	kill	skill
cat	scat	etch	sketch
kin	skin	cab	scab
scale	skip	scare	

He can skip and sketch with skill.

He skated and fell and cut his skin. Then he got a scab.

Kate scared the cat and it scaled the wall.

Writing Sentences

Copy the sentence. Make sure to leave space between the words.

We expect him to fix his box.

....

_____

....

_____

....

_____

Geometry

2 + 2 =   7 − 4 =   3 + 5 =

This is a circle.   Draw your own circle.
It has no sides.

s

scan	scab	scat
scale	scare	skate
skit	skin	skip
skill	skill-fully	
smile	smell	smash
smock	smear	
snob	snot	
snip	snap	snub
spare	spit	spot
sputter	spud	
stop	stun	stab
steep	still	

I can skillfully sketch in steep spots.

I still skip the scary parts.

Writing Words

Write these words: she, shellfish, shelves, Sherry, shopping, shut.

Geometry

5 + 2 =   7 − 5 =   3 + 3 =

This is a triangle.
It has three sides.

Draw your own triangle.

R Blends

ra	bra	brass	Brad	bran
ra	cra	crab	cram	crack
ra	dra	drag	drat	drab
re	fre	Fred	fret	fresh
ri	gri	grip	grill	grit
ro	pro	prop	prom	prod
ru	tru	truck	trum-pet-ing	

I hear the animals trumpeting.

There is a fox trapped inside the grill.

This truck delivers bricks. (de-liv-ers)

Cracked, fresh crab is yummy.

Drag the brass bed up here.

Writing Sentences

Copy the sentence. Make sure to leave space between the words.

I am shining my ship.

Geometry

5 + 4 =   8 − 5 =   3 + 4 =

This is a rectangle.   Draw your own rectangle.
It has four sides.

R Blends

Clear a spot for me at the trading post.

Be cheerful, not grumpy.

Bring lots of creamy treats, please.

He has a trick up his sleeve.

We were at this evening's program.

Grab a blade of green grass.

I am in the bathtub dripping wet.

Black is not the same as white.

We planned a free trip for Fred.

Grandma told me that creaking bones mean bad weather.

I had a dream that I was a crab.

Writing Words

Write these words: cheap, checkers, chips, chapped, chattering, chased.

Geometry

4 + 2 =   7 – 4 =   2 + 3 =

This is a diamond.
It has four sides.

Draw your own diamond.

school   even   three   room   small   book

teacher   noon   rude   reading   poor

It is noon, and the school is out. Do you see the children at play? Some run and jump, some play ball, and three little girls play school under a tree.

What a big room for such a small school! Mary is the teacher. They all have books in their hands, and Tammy is reading. They are all good girls and would not be rude even in playing school. Kate and Mary listen to Tammy as she reads from her book.

What do you think she is reading about? I will tell you. It is about a poor little boy who was lost in the woods.

When Tammy has finished, the three girls will go home. In a little while, too, the boys will stop playing.

Writing Sentences

Copy the sentence. Make sure to leave space between the words.

The teacher checked the tests.

Word Problems

If you had four tropical fish in your tank and bought four more fish from the store, how many fish would you have all together? You could draw a picture to help you find the answer.

If you had a box of eight markers and took out three of them, how many would be left in the box? You could draw a picture to help you find the answer.

Review

Glitter is fun to put on crafts.

Slithering snakes like cramped muddy spots. (Sli-ther-ing)

I like to eat snacks between meals.

Bring trunks to pack for the trip to the tropics. (trop-ics)

Greedy kids do not get treats.

Sniff and smell this rose.

Grab a clock and time me!

She pricked her finger and it bled.

The clearing was cleaned for a picnic.

Writing Sentences

Copy the sentence. Make sure to leave space between the words.

Why is the weather so cold?

Word Problems

If you had five cats and brought home three birds, how many pets would you have all together? You could draw a picture to help you find the answer.

If you had five beans on your plate and ate two of them, how many would be left on your plate? You could draw a picture to help you find the answer.

AR

are	bar	car	far	par	tar
art	bark	card	farm	park	tarp
arm	cart	part	tart		
dart	mart	start	smart		
darn	yarn	barn	harm		
dark	hark	mark	stark	spark	

sparkles

That was sharp! Be careful.

The bug darted here and there.

Tree bark can be made into paper.

He can hear barking on a farm.

Are we going to the park?

Pull the cart along with us.

Pride can be harmful.

Writing Sentences

Copy the sentence. Make sure to leave space between the words.

There is the thin path that leads home.

_____

_____

_____

_____

_____

_____

Word Problems

If you had five friends coming to dinner and their two parents were coming with them, how many people would be coming over? Can you write the math equation like 1 + 2 = 3?

If you had seven crackers and shared four of them, how many would you have left? Can you write the math equation, something like 4 - 2 = 2?

OR

or	for	ford	fork	fort	form
cord	cork	sort	pork	bore	horse
horn	corn	torn	born		

The E is silent in horse. There is no vowel near it for the E to change its sound.

These sound the same but are AR words:

war   wart   warm

warp   ward   warn

There is going to be a storm warning.

Was he born in September? (Sep-tem-ber)

The corn has ripened; we can begin picking.

She eats pork with a fork.

A horn is a brass instrument. (in-stru-ment)

I told her that it was boring.

Sort these socks for me, please.

Ride the horse back to the barn.

Writing Sentences

Copy the sentence. Make sure to leave space between the words.

We think we hear a duck quacking.

_____

_____

_____

_____

_____

Word Problems

If you picked five apples and then picked three more, how many would you have all together? Can you write the math equation like 1 + 2 = 3?

If you had four stories to read and had read two already, how many more did you have to read? Can you write the math equation, something like 2 - 1 = 1?

OR

These sound like OR but are spelled differently:

door	floor	more	score
four	your	roar	soar

This sentence has all six different spellings for OR. Can you find them all?

Four stores got awards for selling boards indoors.

After the storm it will be warmer.

There were no scores; it was the most boring game ever.

Wipe your feet before you step on the floor.

It poured in the morning and I was dripping wet.

We walked north while we watched an eagle soar. (Watched has a different A sound. Can you figure it out?)

Writing Sentences

Copy the sentence. Make sure to leave space between the words.

Where is she chasing him so quickly?

Word Problems

Come up with a question that needs you to add or subtract to answer it. Draw a picture to show the question and write the math equation it shows.

apple   mew   tease   cracker   down   new   friends
asleep   wants   calls   knew   silly   upon   flew   landed

Lucy has a new pet. Do you know what kind of bird it is? Lucy calls her Polly.

Polly can say, "Poor Poll! Poor Poll! Polly wants a cracker;" and she can meow like a cat.

But Polly and the cat are not good friends. One day Polly flew down, and landed on the cat's back when she was asleep.

I think she knew the cat would not like that, and she did it to tease her.

When Lucy pets the cat, Polly flies up into the old apple tree, and will not come when she calls her. Then Lucy says, "What a silly bird!"

Writing Words

Write these words: blooper, clapping, slapped, flip, plates, glad.

....

_____

....

_____

....

_____

....

_____

Review

3 + 2 =   9 – 4 =   4 + 3 =

How much are these coins worth? Write the number of cents next to each line of coins. Count by tens and then count on by one and by five.

      _____

      _____

ER IR UR

These sound the same but are spelled differently:

her	herd	perm	perch
bird	dirt	first	thirst
burn	hurt	purr	turn

The girl got hurt falling in the dirt.

The cat slurped milk when she was thirsty.

A bird sat singing from its perch.

Her farm has a herd of pigs.

Be careful not to get burned.

I got a perm, so my hair is curly.

I finished my chores first.

(We haven't learned the word "my" yet. Did you figure out that the Y says I like in why?)

Writing Words

Write these words: cleaner, sleeping, clogged, slipper, cleared, sleds.

....

_____

....

_____

....

_____

Review

$5 + 2 =$ $9 - 4 =$ $4 + 5 =$

How much are these coins worth? Write the number of cents next to each line of coins.

     _____

     _____

More UR Sounds

These words have the same UR sound in them but are spelled in two different ways.

work   word   worm   world
earth   heard   learn   earn

The early bird gets the worm.

I think that was the worst I heard!

The whole world shares the earth.

I finished my chores first.

The girl learned her words this week.

I heard your song being sung at church.

The card got torn at the park.

See you later alligator.
After a while crocodile.

I earn money being a hard worker.

Writing Sentences

Copy the sentence. Make sure to leave space between the words.

I am sleepy. Please be quiet so I can go to sleep.

....

_____

....

_____

....

_____

Review

5 + 5 =   8 − 4 =   3 + 2 =

Draw a shape with four sides.

AI

You learned that ee and ea both say E. Well, the rule that "when two vowels go awalking the first one does the talking" is true for other sounds too. We are first going to look at different ways to make the A sound, at different ways to make A say its name. One way is with the letters ai together.

sail	tail	rail	wail
pail	mail	nail	jail
fail	trail	train	rain
pain	gain	main	plain
pair	hair	lair	maid
paid	raid	laid	wait
paint	faint	fair	dainty

Use the pail and paint the plain train rail red.

Deliver the mail quickly to the jail in the rain.

Writing Sentences

Copy the sentence. Make sure to leave space between the words.

She got a smear on her smock.

_____

_____

_____

Time

4 + 3 =   7 – 2 =   5 + 2 =

What time is it? What number is the short hand pointing to?

_____ o'clock

AY

Here's another combination that makes A say its name.

say	ray	may	pay
lay	day	hay	way
away	tray	clay	play
pray	today	holiday	gray

Today is a gray day, but I want to play.

Bring clay on a tray and we'll play.

("We'll" means we will. The apostrophe separates the WE from the Ls. You don't read the word as "well." You read WE and then add the L sound.)

I will pay the way for us on the train.

Let's go away for the holiday.

Pray for a better way.

Saying "please" is polite manners.

She was learning to lay the hay for the animals.

A word to learn with the A sound is they.

Writing Words

Write these words: stepped, still, spitting, sticks, stopped, speedy.

Adding and Subtracting

5 - 2 =   1 + 2 =   5 + 2 =

6 - 3 =   6 + 2 =   5 + 3 =

7 - 4 =   4 + 5 =   3 + 4 =

10 - 5 =   3 + 5 =   5 + 5 =

"Well, children, did you have a nice time in the woods?"

"Oh yes, mother, such a good time! See what sweet flowers we found, and what soft moss. The best flowers are for grandma. Won't they please her?"

"Yes; and it will please grandma to know that you thought of her."

"Spot was such a good dog, mother."

We left him under the big tree by the brook, to take care of the dolls and the basket.

"When we came back, they were all safe. No one could get them while Spot was there." (You can stop here today.)

We gave him some of the crackers from the basket.

"O mother, how the birds did sing in the woods!"

"Tammy said she would like to be a bird and have a nest in a tree. But I think she would want to come home to sleep."

"If she were a bird, her nest would be her home. But what would mother do, I wonder, without her little Tammy?"

Writing Words

Write these words: skill, sketched, skipping, scared, scales, scab.

_____

_____

_____

_____

_____

Adding and Subtracting 2 (Count on and off)

$5 - 2 =$ $1 + 2 =$ $5 + 2 =$

$6 - 2 =$ $6 + 2 =$ $7 - 2 =$

$7 + 2 =$ $2 + 7 =$ $3 - 2 =$

$10 - 2 =$ $9 - 2 =$ $2 + 8 =$

Finish the story. *Shows where you left off.

"Well, children, did you have a nice time in the woods?"

"Oh yes, mother, such a good time! See what sweet flowers we found, and what soft moss. The best flowers are for grandma. Won't they please her?"

"Yes; and it will please grandma to know that you thought of her."

"Spot was such a good dog, mother."

We left him under the big tree by the brook, to take care of the dolls and the basket.

"When we came back, they were all safe. No one could get them while Spot was there."

*We gave him some of the crackers from the basket.

"O mother, how the birds did sing in the woods!"

"Tammy said she would like to be a bird and have a nest in a tree. But I think she would want to come home to sleep."

"If she were a bird, her nest would be her home. But what would mother do, I wonder, without her little Tammy?"

Writing Words

Write these words: still, spotting, stunned, snaps, smash, smelly.

_____

_____

_____

_____

_____

_____

Subtracting to 2 and 1 (If numbers are next to each other on the number line, their difference is 1. If they are two apart, their difference is two.)

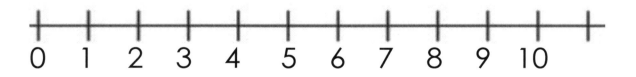

0   1   2   3   4   5   6   7   8   9   10

5 - 4 =   7 - 6 =   5 - 3 =

6 - 5 =   9 - 8 =   9 - 7 =

7 - 5 =   6 - 4 =   3 - 2 =

Long O Sound

Here are some ways that you can write the long O sound, how you can make O say its name.

oat   boat   coat   float   goat

doe   foe   hoe   goes   toe

tow   bow   mow   row   low

know   This has a silent letter K, which keeps it from saying now.

I like yellow roses and he likes bows and arrows.

I know his pillow has boats on it.

The goat eats the grass to mow it!

This floats so slowly.

He goes to play with no coat.

Your toes are in a row.

The doe bends low to eat the oats.

Did they see the rainbow?

Calendar

Fill in the name of the month. Find where 1 belongs and then fill in the day numbers in each day's box.

_____

Sunday	Monday	Tuesday	Wednesday	Thursday	Friday	Saturday

Long O and A Sounds

Row, row, row your boat, gently up the stream. Merrily, merrily, merrily, merrily, life is but a dream. (We haven't used the soft G in gently before.)

We know Little Bo Peep has lost her sheep.

The wind blows softly and the stream flows slowly.

Wait and stay today to play and paint.

Rain, rain go away.

The boat sails swiftly in the sea.

The jam on his toast stained his shirt.

The soap boat floats in the bathtub.

Mowing the grass is my chore.

Yesterday we went below deck.
(yes – ter –day)

Train tracks   chain cracks   stained stacks

Writing Words

Write these words: Fred, brick, props, cracked, dragging, gripped.

_____

_____

_____

_____

_____

Six Plus Three Equals Nine

6 + 3 =   2 + 5 =   4 + 3 =

2 + 4 =   3 + 3 =   3 + 6 =

2 + 6 =   3 + 4 =   3 + 5 =

5 + 3 =   6 + 3 =   4 + 4 =

3 + 6 =   5 + 2 =   2 + 8 =

Long U Sound

Two vowels make the first say its name:

true   glue   blue

fruit   suit

Here's a word that does not follow the rule!   shoe

Here are other ways to make the long U sound.

too	soon	spoon	moon
food	tooth	cartoon	

Ew!	new	pew	blew
flew	stew	chew	mew

you   soup   group

Eat your fruit stew with a spoon.

Do you think it is true that the suit is blue?

These OO words have a different sound. You've seen LOOK. These rhyme with look.

book   took

Writing Sentences

Copy the sentence. Make sure to leave a space between the words.

He has a trick up his sleeves.

....

_____

....

_____

....

_____

Nine Minus Six Equals Three

6 - 3 =	8 - 5 =	9 - 3 =
9 - 4 =	3 - 3 =	9 - 6 =
9 - 6 =	8 - 4 =	7 - 2 =
9 - 3 =	7 - 3 =	4 - 4 =
8 - 6 =	5 - 2 =	9 - 8 =

IE

Here is a weird one. Sometimes IE sounds like the letter name E. There is a spelling rule that requires this. It goes like this: I before E except after C.

field   shield   thief   belief

believe   relieve   Debbie   Katie

You can also see it in some plural words. When a y comes after a vowel we just add an s, like in *day* we write *days* and for *key* we write *keys*. But if the y doesn't come after a vowel, if it comes after a consonant, we write it like this:

party   parties   daisy   daisies

baby   babies   puppy   puppies

The thief stole the daisies.

I know he took them for the parties.

The puppies are playing in the field.

I believe a nap will relieve the babies.

He hung the shield up in the lobby for the tourists to see.

Writing Sentences

Copy the sentence. Make sure to leave a space between the words.

Glitter is fun to put on crafts.

Write: 1, 2, 3, 4, 5

Six Plus Four Equals Ten

6 + 4 =	2 + 5 =	4 + 3 =
4 + 6 =	3 + 3 =	6 + 3 =
2 + 6 =	3 + 4 =	3 + 5 =
3 + 6 =	6 + 4 =	4 + 4 =
3 + 4 =	5 + 2 =	4 + 6 =

IE

Now ie is going to sound the way it should. It is going to make I say its name. It does this at the end of word.

pie   lie   tie

We know Y can sound like E, but it can sound like I too. Basically, when it comes at the end of a short word it will sound like Y and at the end of a long word it will sound like E.

try   tries   fly   flies
fry   fries   pry   pries
spy   spies

He tries so hard to fly.

Try to pry this pie from the pan.

Never tell lies.

Eat these yummy cheesy fries.

There is a fly on my tie.

He trapped the thief by spying on him.

Writing Words

Write these word pairs: arm - farm, ark – bark, art – part, car - card.

_____

_____

_____

_____

Write: 6, 7, 8, 9, 10

_____

Ten Minus Six Equals Four

10 - 6 =   8 - 5 =   6 - 4 =

10 - 4 =   7 - 3 =   10 - 5 =

9 - 6 =   10 - 4 =   10 - 2 =

10 - 6 =   8 - 2 =   9 - 5 =

I sounds

Here are some more words with the I sound.

my	by	type	style
guy	buy		
rye	bye		
guide			
high	light	night	bright

My guide has weird style.

I like rye and wheat but not oat.

Go spy on that guy.

Why are you so shy?

I believe Debbie tries to type super fast.

Hang the light up high by the daisies over there so that it will be bright tonight in here.

My kids are playing hide and seek.

Writing Words

Write these word pairs: for - Ford, or – horn, war – warm, fork - fort.

Write: 11, 12, 13, 14, 15

Six Plus Five Equals Eleven

6 + 5 =   2 + 5 =   4 + 3 =

4 + 6 =   3 + 3 =   6 + 5 =

2 + 6 =   3 + 4 =   5 + 6 =

3 + 4 =   5 + 6 =   6 + 4 =

Long Vowel Sounds

The tiny bird tries to fly free in the air. I see its first flight.

Coal is burned in stoves for heat.

This new book has interesting stories.

I believe this daisy field is for sale.

People think that trees grow slowly.

May we please use the guidebook?

The boat will be waiting in the harbor tonight.

Type this word as quickly as you can.

Flour and sugar together make yummy muffins.

Your chore is to rake and pile the leaves.

Sue buys stew and pie for lunch.

Writing Sentences

Copy the sentence. Make sure to leave space between the words.

Four stores get awards for selling floor boards.

Write: 16, 17, 18, 19, 20

Eleven Minus Six Equals Five

$11 - 6 =$ $11 - 5 =$ $6 - 2 =$

$10 - 4 =$ $7 - 4 =$ $10 - 5 =$

$11 - 5 =$ $10 - 4 =$ $10 - 6 =$

$9 - 3 =$ $8 - 4 =$ $9 - 6 =$

If you start to have trouble as the numbers get bigger, you could make yourself a number line that you keep with your math book. Write numbers two through eighteen on it. (It doesn't have to have a line, just the numbers.)

CE

Today we are going to read C words, words that are written CE. When C is followed by E (or I or Y) it sounds like an S instead of K. Here are some words to read.

ice	rice	mice	nice
spice	twice	slice	price
space	race	face	place
prince	France	dance	
cement	cell	celebrate	celery

Is France a leader in the space race?

Use that spice twice to make the rice.

Let's dance to celebrate!

Pour the cement into place.

Paint the kids' faces like mice.

Writing Sentences

Copy the sentence. Make sure to leave space between the words.

The girl got hurt falling in the dirt.

Write: 21, 22, 23, 24, 25

Seven Plus Three Equals Ten

7 + 3 =	3 + 5 =	2 + 3 =
4 + 6 =	3 + 3 =	6 + 5 =
4 + 5 =	3 + 7 =	5 + 4 =
3 + 6 =	7 + 3 =	6 + 2 =
3 + 7 =	5 + 6 =	6 + 4 =

beach   shells   these   seat   waves   going

ever   sea   watch   evening   lazy   side

These boys and girls live near the sea. They have been to the beach. It is now evening, and they are going home.

John, who sits on the front seat, found some pretty shells. They are in the basket by his side.

Ben White is driving. He holds the lines in one hand and his whip in the other.

Robert has his hat in his hand, and is looking at the horses. He thinks they are very lazy; they do not trot fast.

The children are not far from home. In a little while the sun will set, and it will be bedtime.

Have you ever been at the seaside? Do you like to watch the big waves and to play on the wet sand?

Writing Sentences

Copy the sentence. Make sure to leave space between the words.

The early bird gets the worm.

....

_____

....

_____

Write: 26, 27, 28, 29, 30

_____

Ten Minus Seven Equals Three

$10 - 7 =$ $11 - 5 =$ $6 - 2 =$

$10 - 4 =$ $7 - 3 =$ $10 - 7 =$

$10 - 3 =$ $8 - 6 =$ $10 - 6 =$

$9 - 5 =$ $10 - 3 =$ $9 - 6 =$

$11 - 6 =$ $7 - 5 =$ $9 - 4 =$

CI, CY

Here are more words where C sounds like S. Why does E come before I in received? I before E except after C is the rule.

circle   circus   cycle   cyclone

cylinder (sill – in – der)   city

More words:

receive   ceiling   receipt
                              (The P is silent.)

Do you see what's in the center circle ring at the circus?

Did you receive a receipt from the waiter?

The hot air floats to the ceiling and cools and then falls down again in a cycle.

That's a fancy dance she performed.

The lights in the city are bright.

I ride my bicycle to the park.

Writing Words

Write these word pairs: rain – main, hair – fair, maid – paid, sail - tail.

_____

_____

_____

_____

_____

_____

Write: 31, 32, 33, 34, 35

_____

Seven Plus Four Equals Eleven

7 + 4 =   3 + 5 =   6 + 4 =

4 + 7 =   5 + 3 =   6 + 5 =

4 + 5 =   4 + 7 =   5 + 4 =

3 + 7 =   5 + 6 =   7 + 4 =

log   quiet   proud   pulled   fish   stump   river   father

One evening Frank's father said to him, "Frank, would you like to go with me to catch some fish?"

"Yes; may I go with you, father?"

"Yes, Frank, you may go with me."

"That would make me happy!"

Here they are on the bank of a river. Frank has just pulled a fine fish out of the water. How proud he feels!

See what a nice, quiet spot they have found. Frank has the stump of a big tree for his seat, and his father sits on a log nearby. They like the sport.

Writing Words

Write these word pairs: gray – pray, day – today, say - way, play – clay.

Write: 36, 37, 38, 39, 40

Eleven Minus Seven Equals Four

11 - 7 =	11 - 5 =	11 - 7 =
11 - 4 =	8 - 3 =	10 - 3 =
9 - 5 =	10 - 7 =	9 - 6 =
11 - 6 =	8 - 5 =	11 - 4 =

What two letters do all the underlined words have in common?
What sound do they make when they are together?

boy   our   <u>spoil</u>   hurrah   own   <u>coil</u>   <u>noise</u>   fourth

such   <u>join</u>   thank   about   <u>hoist</u>   pay   July   playing

"Papa, may we have the big flag?" said James.

"What can my little boy do with such a big flag?"

"Hoist it on our tent, papa. We are playing Fourth of July."

"Is that what all this noise is about? Why not hoist your own flags?"

"Oh! They are too little."

"You might spoil my flag."

"Then we will all join to pay for it. But we will not spoil it, papa."

"Take it, then, and take the coil of rope with it."

"Oh! Thank you."

Writing Words

Write these word pairs: coat - boat, low – below, oat – float, toe – goes.

_____

_____

_____

_____

_____

_____

Write: 41, 42, 43, 44, 45

_____

Seven Plus Five Equals Twelve

7 + 5 =   3 + 4 =   6 + 2 =

4 + 5 =   4 + 7 =   5 + 7 =

5 + 6 =   7 + 5 =   3 + 6 =

5 + 7 =   5 + 2 =   7 + 4 =

sled   throw   winter   hurt   ice   cover   Henry   next
skate   ground   mercy   snow   sister   laughing   pair

I like winter, when snow and ice cover the ground. What fun it is to throw snowballs, and to skate on the ice!

See the boys and girls! How merry they are! Henry has his sled, and draws his little sister. There they go!

I think Henry is kind; his sister is too small to skate.

Look! Did you see that boy fall down? But I see he is not hurt, for he is laughing.

Some other boys have just come to join in the fun. See them put on their skates.

Henry says, that he hopes his father will get a pair of skates for his sister next winter.

Writing Sentences

Copy the sentence. Make sure to leave a space between the words.

The wind blows softly and the stream flows slowly.

_____

_____

_____

_____

Write: 46, 47, 48, 49, 50

_____

Twelve Minus Seven Equals Five

11 - 7 =	11 - 5 =	12 - 7 =
11 - 4 =	10 - 4 =	10 - 3 =
10 - 3 =	10 - 6 =	12 - 7 =
12 - 5 =	10 - 7 =	9 - 6 =
11 - 6 =	8 - 4 =	12 - 5 =

paw   polite   means   isn't   speak   sir   shake

Fido   tricks   teach   dinner   Ellen   bowwow

Ellen, look at Fido! He sits up in a chair, with my hat on. He looks like a little boy; but it is only Fido.

Now see him shake hands. Give me your paw, Fido. How do you do, sir? Will you have dinner with us. Fido? Speak! Fido says, "Bowwow," which means, "Thank you, I will."

Isn't Fido a good dog, Ellen? He is always so polite. When school is out, I will try to teach him some other tricks.

Writing Words

Copy the sentence. Make sure to leave a space between the words.

Eat your fruit stew with a spoon.

_____

_____

Write: 51, 52, 53, 54, 55

_____

Eight Plus Three Equals Eleven

$4 + 7 =$ $3 + 7 =$ $3 + 8 =$

$4 + 5 =$ $5 + 6 =$ $6 + 7 =$

$6 + 4 =$ $8 + 3 =$ $2 + 8 =$

$8 + 3 =$ $3 + 4 =$ $5 + 3 =$

$4 + 4 =$ $6 + 3 =$ $2 + 5 =$

shed pain way stole saw hid eat Nero Hattie
suffer sorry something caught tried

"O Hattie! I just saw a large rat in the shed; and old Nero tried to catch it."

"Did he catch it, Frank?"

"No; Nero did not; but the old cat did."

"My cat?"

"No, it was the other one."

"Do tell me how she got it, Frank. Did she run after it?"

"No, that was not the way. Nero hid on a big box. The rat stole out, and she jumped at it and caught it."

"Poor rat! It must have been very hungry; it came out to get something to eat."

"Why, Hattie, you are not sorry she got the rat, are you?"

"No, I cannot say I am sorry she got it; but I do not like to see even a rat suffer pain."

Writing Words

Write these words on the lines: believe, field, parties, thief, puppies.

_____

_____

_____

_____

Write: 56, 57, 58, 59, 60

_____

Eleven Minus Eight Equals Three

10 - 7 =   9 - 6 =   11 - 7 =

11 - 8 =   10 - 6 =   11 - 3 =

11 - 3 =   12 - 5 =   3 - 2 =

10 - 4 =   9 - 7 =   11 - 8 =

12 - 7 =   11 - 6 =   10 - 5 =

roll   build   grandpa   hard   foam   ships
houses   long   sail   break   wooden   blow

Mary and Lucy have come down to the beach with their grandpa. They live in a town near the sea.

Their grandpa likes to sit on the large rock and watch the big ships as they sail far away on the blue sea. Sometimes he sits there all day long.

The little girls like to dig in the sand and pick up pretty shells. They watch the waves as they roll up on the beach and break into white foam.

They sometimes make little houses of sand and build walls around them, and they dig wells with their small wooden spades.

They have been picking up shells for their little sister. She is too young to come to the beach.

I think all children like to play by the seaside when the sun is bright and the wind does not blow too hard.

Writing Words

Write these word pairs on the lines: spy – spies, try – tries, lie - tie, fly – flies.

Write: 61, 62, 63, 64, 65

Eight Plus Four Equals Twelve

4 + 6 =   5 + 5 =   8 + 3 =

4 + 8 =   5 + 3 =   7 + 5 =

3 + 8 =   8 + 4 =   4 + 7 =

8 + 4=   4 + 3 =   7 + 2 =

asked   wanted   four   Willie's   night   rabbits
lad   carried   cents   telling   fifty   master

One day, Willie's father saw a boy at the market with four little white rabbits in a basket.

He thought these would be nice pets for Willie; so he asked the lad how much he wanted for his rabbits.

The boy said, "Only fifty cents, sir."

Willie's father bought them, and carried them home.

Here you see the rabbits and their little master. He has a pen for them, and always shuts them in it at night to keep them safe.

He gives them bread and grass to eat. They like grass, and will take it from his hand. He has called in a little friend to see them.

Willie is telling him about their funny ways.

Writing Words

Write these words on the lines: light, type, by, goodbye, buying.

_____

_____

_____

_____

Write: 66, 67, 68, 69, 70

_____

Twelve Minus Eight Equals Four

12 - 4 =   9 - 6 =   12 - 7 =

11 - 3 =   12 - 4 =   8 - 3 =

10 - 4 =   10 - 7 =   12 - 8 =

12 - 8 =   11 - 6 =   4 - 1 =

bush   cunning   place   show   find

broken   over   bring   again   fasten

"Come here, Rose. Look down into this bush."

"O Willie! A bird's nest! What cunning, little eggs! May we take it and show it to mother?"

"What would the old bird do, Rose, if she should come back and not find her nest?"

"Oh, we would bring it right back, Willie!"

"Yes, but we could not fasten it in its place again. If the wind blows it over, the eggs would get broken."

Writing Words

Copy the sentence carefully. Leave space between the words.

The boat will be waiting in the harbor tonight.

Write: 71, 72, 73, 74, 75

Eight Plus Five Equals Thirteen

4 + 6 =   7 + 5 =   8 + 3 =

4 + 8 =   7 + 3 =   6 + 5 =

5 + 8 =   8 + 5 =   4 + 7 =

8 + 4=   6 + 3 =   7 + 2 =

8 + 5 =   5 + 6 =   3 + 7 =

strong   round   dry   bill   worked
sends   claws   flit   God   spring

"How does the bird make the nest so strong, Willie?"

"The mother bird has her bill and her claws to work with, but she would not know how to make the nest if God did not teach her. Do you see what it is made of?"

"Yes, Willie, I see some horse-hairs and some dry grass. The old bird must have worked hard to find all the hairs, and make them into such a pretty, round nest."

"Should we take the nest, Rose?"

"Oh no, Willie! We must not take it; but we will come and look at it again, some time."

Writing Words

Copy the sentence carefully. Leave space between the words.

Use that spice twice to make the rice.

Write: 76, 77, 78, 79, 80

Thirteen Minus Eight Equals Five

13 - 8 =   9 - 6 =   12 - 7 =

11 - 8 =   13 - 5 =   11 - 7 =

11 - 3 =   12 - 5 =   12 - 4 =

10 - 4 =   10 - 7 =   13 - 8 =

13 - 5 =   11 - 6 =   12 - 8 =

feathers   ago   fly   worm   crumb   feeding
ugly   off   feed   brown   guess   things

"Willie, when I was feeding the birds just now, a little brown bird flew away with a crumb in its bill."

"Where did it go, Rose?"

"I don't know; away off, somewhere."

"I can guess where, Rose. Don't you know the nest we saw some days ago? What do you think is in it now?"

"O Willie, I know! Some little brown birds. Let us go and see them."

(to be continued…)

Writing Words

Copy the sentence carefully. Leave space between the words.

Do you see what's in the center circle ring at the circus?

Write: 81, 82, 83, 84, 85

Word Problems

Thirteen kids were at the party. After eight left, how many kids were still at the party?

There were ten dogs at the pound. Three were chosen and taken home in one day. How many were left at the pound?

Finish the story. *Marks where you left off.

"Willie, when I was feeding the birds just now, a little brown bird flew away with a crumb in its bill."

"Where did it go, Rose?"

"I don't know; away off, somewhere."

"I can guess where, Rose. Don't you know the nest we saw some days ago? What do you think is in it now?"

"O Willie, I know! Some little brown birds. Let us go and see them."

*"All right; but we must not go too near. There! I just saw the old bird fly out of the bush. Stand here, Rose. Can you see?"

"Why, Willie, what ugly little things! What big mouths they have, and no feathers!"

"Keep still, Rose. Here comes the old bird with a worm in her bill. How hard she must work to feed them all!"

Day 163

Writing Words

Write your whole name.

Write: 86, 87, 88, 89, 90

Patterns

Jeremy had eleven fish in his tank. Jeremy gave away five to friends. How many fish were left in Jeremy's tank?

Write the next number in the pattern.

21, 31, 41, 51, 61, 71, _____

whistle   pocket   willow   note   filled   dead   sick
walk   every   blew   lane   lame   taking   cane   took

One day, when Mary was taking a walk down the lane, try-ing to sing her doll to sleep, she met Frank, with his basket and cane.

Frank was a poor, little, lame boy. His father and mother were dead. His dear, old grandma took care of him, and tried to make him happy.

Every day, Mary's mother filled Frank's basket with bread and meat, and a little tea for his grandma.

(You can stop here today.)

"How do you do, Frank?" said Mary. "Don't make a noise; my doll is going to sleep. It is just a little sick to-day."

"Well, then, let us whistle it to sleep." And Frank, taking a willow whistle out of his pocket, blew a long note.

"Oh, how sweet!" cried Mary. "Do let me try."

Writing Words

Write your address.

_____

_____

_____

Write: 91, 92, 93, 94, 95

_____

Patterns

There were twelve balloons at the party. Four of them popped.
How many were left that were not popped?

Write the next two numbers in the pattern.

10, 20, 10, 30, 10, 40, 10, 50, _____

Finish the story. *Marks where you left off.

whistle   pocket   willow   note   filled   dead   sick
walk   every   blew   lane   lame   taking   cane   took

One day, when Mary was taking a walk down the lane, try-ing to sing her doll to sleep, she met Frank, with his basket and cane.

Frank was a poor, little, lame boy. His father and mother were dead. His dear, old grandma took care of him, and tried to make him happy.

Every day, Mary's mother filled Frank's basket with bread and meat, and a little tea for his grandma.

*"How do you do, Frank?" said Mary. "Don't make a noise; my doll is going to sleep. It is just a little sick today."

"Well, then, let us whistle it to sleep." And Frank, taking a willow whistle out of his pocket, blew a long note.

"Oh, how sweet!" cried Mary. "Do let me try."

Writing Words

Write an "I love you" note to someone.

_____

_____

_____

Write: 96, 97, 98, 99, 100

_____

Patterns

Peter won twelve prizes and he gave three prizes to his friend. How many prizes did he still have?

Write the next two numbers in the pattern.

58, 56, 54, 52, 50, 48, 46, 44, _____

turned   face   cried   low   almost
soon   more   cry   once   because

"Yes, Mary, I will give it to you, because you are so good to my grandma."

"Oh! Thank you very much." Mary blew and blew a long time. "I can't make it whistle," said she, almost ready to cry.

"Sometimes they will whistle, and sometimes they won't," said Frank. "Try again, Mary."

She tried once more, and the whistle made a low, sweet sound. "It whistles!" she cried.

(to be continued...)

Writing Numbers

Practice writing your phone number.

_____

_____

_____

_____

_____

Patterns

Two girls were picking flowers. One gathered up four and the other gathered up eight. How many flowers did they have all together?

What comes next? (Hint: How many sides would the next shape have?)

Finish the story. *Marks where you left off.

"Yes, Mary, I will give it to you, because you are so good to my grandma."

"Oh! Thank you very much." Mary blew and blew a long time. "I can't make it whistle," said she, almost ready to cry.

"Sometimes they will whistle, and sometimes they won't," said Frank. "Try again, Mary."

She tried once more, and the whistle made a low, sweet sound. "It whistles!" she cried.

*In her joy, she had turned the doll's face down, and its eyes shut tight, as if it had gone to sleep.

"There!" cried Frank, "I told you the way to put a doll to sleep, is to whistle to it."

"So it is," said Mary. "Dear, little thing; it must be put in its bed now."

So they went into the house. Frank's basket was soon filled, and he went home happy.

Writing

Write you city, state (providence), and country.

....

_____

....

_____

....

_____

....

_____

Patterns

If there were three squirrels, two chipmunks, and one groundhog in the yard, how many animals were there?

Write the next number in the pattern.

12, 23, 34, 45, 56, 67, 78, _____

stood   himself   flapping   first   twelve   flapped
walked   flap   obey   better   Chippy   food
stone   before   chickens   kept

There was once a big hen that had twelve little chickens. They were very small, and the old hen took good care of them. She found food for them in the daytime, and at night kept them under her wings.

One day, this old hen took her chickens down to a small brook. She thought the air from the water would do them good.

When they got to the brook, they walked on the bank a little while. It was very pretty on the other side of the brook, and the old hen thought she would take her children over there.

(to be continued…)

Writing

Write, "I am _____ years old." Fill in how old you are!

_____

_____

_____

_____

Subtracting

6 - 4 =   9 - 6 =   12 - 7 =

11 - 3 =   12 - 4 =   8 - 3 =

10 - 4 =   10 - 7 =   12 - 8 =

9 - 8 =   11 - 6 =   11 - 2 =

Finish the story.

There was a large stone in the brook. She thought it would be easy for them to jump to that stone, and from it to the other side.

So she jumped to the stone, and told the children to come after her. For the first time, she found that they would not obey her.

She flapped her wings, and cried, "Come here, all of you! Jump up on this stone, as I did. We can then jump to the other side. Come now!"

"O mother! We can't, we can't, we can't!" said all the little chickens.

"Yes you can, if you try," said the old hen. "Just flap your wings, as I did, and you can jump over."

"I am flapping my wings," said Chippy, who stood by himself; "but I can't jump any better than I could before."

Writing

Write the names of your siblings (or cousins).

_____

_____

_____

_____

_____

Adding

6 + 5 =	5 + 2 =	4 + 3 =
2 + 8 =	4 + 6 =	3 + 7 =
5 + 8 =	8 + 3 =	4 + 8 =
3 + 6 =	5 + 7 =	7 + 4 =

This is your last page like this. It's okay if you still need lots of practice to get these down. I hope you are good at figuring out the answers and getting your work done cheerfully and without a lot of delay.

chirped never indeed slowly really brood
began didn't use door bite piece

"I never saw such children," said the old hen. "You don't try at all."

"We can't jump so far, mother. Indeed we can't, we can't!" chirped the little chickens.

"Well," said the old hen, "I must give it up." So she jumped back to the bank, and walked slowly home with her brood.

"I think mother asked too much of us," said one little chicken to the others.

(to be continued...)

Writing

Write your parents' names.

_____

_____

_____

_____

_____

What's 6 + 6, 7 + 7, 8 + 8 and 9 + 9?
Find the pattern. Count to check your answer.

$0 + 0 =$ $5 + 5 =$

$1 + 1 =$ $6 + 6 =$

$2 + 2 =$ $7 + 7 =$

$3 + 3 =$ $8 + 8 =$

$4 + 4 =$ $9 + 9 =$

Finish the story.

chirped   never   indeed   slowly   really   brood
began   didn't   use   door   bite   piece

"Well, I tried," said Chippy.

"We didn't," said the others; "it was of no use to try."

When they got home, the old hen began to look about for something to eat. She soon found, near the back door, a piece of bread.

So she called the chickens, and they all ran up to her, each one trying to get a bite at the piece of bread.

"No, no!" said the old hen. "This bread is for Chippy. He is the only one of my children that really tried to jump to the stone."

Day 171

Write the name of a story. Names start with a capital
letter.

_____

_____

Count to 100 and fill in the missing numbers.

1	2		4	5	6	7		9	10
11		13	14	15		17	18	19	20
21	22	23		25	26	27	28		30
31	32	33	34	35	36	37	38	39	
41	42	43	44		46	47	48	49	50
	52	53	54	55	56		58	59	60
61	62		64	65	66	67	68	69	70
71		73	74	75		77	78	79	80
81	82		84	85	86	87	88		90
	92	93		95	96	97		99	100

last   slates   write   waste   neat   taken
clean   learn   reader   parents   second

We have come to the last lesson in this book. We have finished the First Reader.

You can now read all the lessons in it, and can write them on your slates.

Have you taken good care of your book? Children should always keep their books neat and clean.

Are you not glad to be ready for a new book?

Your parents are very kind to send you to school. If you are good, and if you try to learn, your teacher will love you, and you will please your parents.

Be kind to all, and do not waste your time in school. When you go home, you may ask your parents to get you a Second Reader.

Day 172

Writing

Write a story (or about a story). Read your story.

....

_____

_____

....

_____

_____

....

_____

_____

Coins

3 + 5 =   9 – 5 =   3 + 3 =

How much are these coins worth? Write the number of cents next to each line of coins. Count by tens and then count on by one and by five.

     _____

     _____

Writing

Write a story (or about a story). Read your story.

_____

_____

_____

_____

Coins

8 + 2 =   10 − 5 =   9 + 3 =

How much are these coins worth? Write the number of cents next to each line of coins. Count by tens and then count on by five and by one.

    _____

Writing

Write a story (or about a story). Read your story.

_____

_____

_____

_____

_____

_____

Time

2 + 5 =   9 – 4 =   3 + 5 =

What time is it? What number is the short hand pointing to?

_____ o'clock

Writing

Write a story (or about a story). Read your story.

_____

_____

_____

_____

Time

$4 + 5 =$ $\qquad$ $9 - 2 =$ $\qquad$ $7 + 5 =$

What time is it? What number is
the short hand pointing to?

_____ o'clock

<u>Day 176</u>

Writing

Write a story (or about a story). Read your story.

....

_____

....

_____

....

_____

....

_____

Geometry

6 + 6 =   4 – 1 =   7 + 4 =

Draw a shape with four sides. What is it?

Writing

Write a story (or about a story). Read your story.

_____

_____

_____

_____

Geometry

14 − 6 =   12 − 4 =   3 + 7 =

Draw a shape with three sides. What is it?

Writing

Write a story (or about a story). Read your story.

_____

_____

_____

_____

_____

Patterns

4 + 6 =   11 − 3 =   7 + 5 =

Create a pattern.

Writing

Write a story (or about a story). Read your story.

_____

_____

_____

_____

_____

_____

Patterns

$5 + 7 =$ $14 - 9 =$ $13 - 6 =$

Create a pattern.

Writing

Write a story (or about a story). Read your story.

....

_____

....

_____

....

_____

....

_____

Patterns

Can you figure out the pattern? What are the answers?

9 + 1 =   10 − 9 =

9 + 2 =   11 − 9 =

9 + 3 =   12 − 9 =

9 + 4 =   13 − 9 =

9 + 5 =   14 − 9 =

9 + 6 =   15 − 9 =

9 + 7 =   16 − 9 =

9 + 8 =   17 − 9 =

9 + 9 =   18 − 9 =

I hope you are enjoying learning with Genesis Curriculum. It's time to move on to the main curriculum! You might want to consider using the tracing book next, as it will help with the spelling words in the main curriculum and will help them understand the vocabulary words. They can also use the lines in the tracing book for their sentences for writing.

A Mind for Math allows students from about first through fourth grade to do their daily math together. There are 100 days of lessons with word problems and applications all coming from the daily Bible reading in the main curriculum. Students each have a leveled workbook with 180 days to complete.

On our site you can learn about our curriculum which uses books of the Bible to lead your family through lessons in science, history, language arts, and Biblical languages. We also offer reading resources and learning-together elementary math courses.

GenesisCurriculum.com

Made in the USA
Lexington, KY
20 May 2019